Religion
and Life

FIFTH EDITION
Foundation Edition

Victor W. Watton

Religion and Life

FIFTH EDITION
Foundation Edition

For photo credits and acknowledgments, please see page 144.

Hachette UK's policy is to use papers that are natural, renewable and recyclable products and made from wood grown in sustainable forests. The logging and manufacturing processes are expected to conform to the environmental regulations of the country of origin.

Orders: please contact Bookpoint Ltd, 130 Milton Park, Abingdon, Oxon OX14 4SB. Telephone: (44) 01235 827720. Fax: (44) 01235 400454. Lines are open 9.00–5.00, Monday to Saturday, with a 24-hour message answering service. Visit our website at www.hoddereducation.co.uk

Second edition published (1999)
Third edition published (2001)
Fourth edition published (2005)
This fifth edition published (2009)

Impression number   5 4 3 2 1
Year   2013 2012 2011 2010 2009

Cover photos *l–r*: © Royal Observatory, Edinburgh/AATB/Science Photo Library; © Reuters/Corbis; © Digital Art/Corbis.
Illustrations by Ian Foulis, Daedalus and Barking Dog
Typeset in Electra LH Regular 12pt
Printed in Italy

A catalogue record for this title is available from the British Library.

ISBN: 978 0340 975 480

Religion and Life, Fifth edition: 978 0340 975 473
Religion and Life Teacher's Resource Book Pack, Fifth edition: 978 0340 975 503
Religion and Life Dynamic Learning Network CD-ROM, Second edition: 978 0340 986 806
Religion and Life Revision Guide, Third edition: 978 0340 975 558

Contents

Section 3 **Marriage and the family**

Section 4 **Religion and community cohesion**

Introduction

This book covers all aspects of the Edexcel GCSE Religious Studies Unit 1: Religion and Life based on the study of Christianity and at least one other religion. This GCSE aims to get you to think about yourself, the society in which you live and the meaning of life.

- Each section of the book is a section of the GCSE specification, and the topics cover every part of that section. The main body of the text gives you all the information you need for each topic. The sources in the margin give you extra information for greater understanding of the topic.
- In the examination, you will have to answer one question on Section 1, one question on Section 2, one question on Section 3 and one question on Section 4.
- Wherever the symbol ⓒ occurs at the top of the page, it means that the topic also covers Key Stage 4 Citizenship. Your lesson might therefore also be a citizenship lesson.
- The word God is used throughout the religions so that you understand that names such as Allah and the Almighty are referring to the same God. Where dates are given, CE (Common Era) and BCE (Before the Common Era) are used to remove connections to one particular religion.

How to use the book

- Work through each topic. Words that you might not understand are in bold type so that you can look up their meanings in the relevant glossary at the end of the book (there is a glossary for general words, one for Christian words, one for Muslim words, one for Jewish words, one for Hindu words and one for Sikh words).
- Answer the questions at the end of the topic. For each topic there are examples of b, c and d questions and an exam tip on how to answer one of them. The exam tip gives you hints as to the approach that will gain you full marks. At the end of each section are examples and comments on all types of questions, a–d.
- You should study all the topics in section 1, but in sections 2, 3 and 4, *for the topics that cover Islam, Judaism, Hinduism and Sikhism, you only need to study one of these religions.*

I hope you enjoy your study of Religion and Life. Remember, Religious Studies is not about making you religious, it is about enabling you to think for yourself about religious and moral issues.

Section 1 **Believing in God**

Introduction

This section of the examination specification requires you to look at the issues surrounding belief in God based on the study of one religion.

Reasons why people believe in God
You will need to understand the effects of, and give reasons for your own opinion about:
- a religious upbringing
- religious experience
- the design argument
- the argument from causation.

Reasons why some people do not believe in God
You will need to understand the effects of, and give reasons for your own opinion about:
- scientific explanations of the origins of the world
- unanswered prayers
- evil and suffering.

How Christians respond to the problems
You will need to understand the effects of, and give reasons for your own opinion about how Christians respond to:
- scientific explanations of the world
- unanswered prayers
- the problems of evil and suffering.

The media and belief in God
You will need to understand the effects of, and give reasons for your own opinion about how a television or radio programme about religion could affect attitudes to belief in God.

Topic 1.1 Religious upbringing

There are many reasons for believing in God. Some people are led to believe in God by one reason only, others by a number of reasons.

You only need to know about a religious upbringing in one religion. This topic looks at a Christian religious upbringing. If you know a lot about another religion you could use that instead.

The main features of a Christian upbringing

- Christian parents are likely to have their babies baptised. They promise to bring up their children to believe in God and be good Christians.
- Christian parents teach their children to pray to God.
- Christian parents take their children to worship God in church.
- Christian parents send their children to Sunday School to learn about God and Christianity.
- Christian parents may send their children to a church school.
- Christian parents are likely to encourage their children to be confirmed. This **sacrament of confirmation** may involve a **religious experience** as the child may feel the presence of God in the **prayers**, **vows** and **anointing**.

Minister: *You have brought this child to be baptised ... I ask you therefore:*

Will you provide for this your child a Christian home of love and **faithfulness?**

Parents: *With God's help, we will.*

From the Baptismal Service of the Methodist Church

Holy **baptism** *is the basis of the whole Christian life ... Through baptism we are freed from sin and reborn as sons of God; we become members of Christ, are incorporated into the Church and made sharers in her mission.*

Catechism of the Catholic Church 1213

Why might being confirmed lead to, or support, belief in God?

How a religious upbringing may lead to, or support, belief in God

If you have had a Christian religious upbringing, it is natural to believe in God because:

- Christian parents will have told their children about God. The children will believe their parents.
- Christians pray to God. Children will believe that God exists because their parents would not waste their time praying to nothing.
- Seeing so many people worshipping God at church will make children believe God exists.
- At Sunday or Church school Christian children will be taught that God exists. Children will believe what their teachers tell them is true.
- Before they are confirmed, children will be taught about God and may feel his presence in the service.

*I am a **Catholic** Christian because I was born to Catholic parents, and I was educated in a Catholic school. All my upbringing made me believe in God, and I have never really thought that God might not exist. God is a part of my life just as my parents and friends are.*

A Catholic adult

Exam focus

'Explain' questions (part b) are where your Quality of Written Communication is tested, so you should answer these questions in a formal style of English, be careful with your spelling and try to use some specialist vocabulary (in this section baptism, sacrament, prayer, worship, confirmation, bishop would all be specialist vocabulary).

Questions

b Do you think children should follow the same religion as their parents? Give two reasons for your point of view. **4**

c Explain how a religious upbringing can lead to, or support, belief in God. **8**

d 'A religious upbringing forces children to believe in God.'
   i Do you agree? Give reasons for your opinion. **3**
   ii Give reasons why some people may disagree with you. **3**

Exam Tip

c 'Explain' means give reasons. To answer this question you should name four features of a religious upbringing and explain, in two or three sentences for each, how they might lead to belief in God. Remember your Quality of Written Communication will be assessed in your answer, so:
   - be careful with your spelling
   - use sentences and paragraphs
   - do not use bullet points
   - use specialist vocabulary.

SUMMARY

Having a religious upbringing is likely to lead to belief in God because children are taught that God exists and they spend most of their time with people who believe that God exists.

Topic 1.2 Religious experience

KEY WORDS

Conversion – when your life is changed by giving yourself to God.

Miracle – something which seems to break a law of science and makes you think only God could have done it.

Numinous – the feeling of the presence of something greater than you.

Prayer – an attempt to contact God, usually through words.

Religious experience is something which makes people feel God's presence. You need to know four types of religious experience: **numinous**, **conversion**, **miracle** and **prayer**.

1. The numinous

This is a feeling of the presence of God. When people are in a religious building, in a beautiful place or looking up at the stars on a clear night, they may be filled with the awareness that there is something greater than them. They may feel this to be God. If you become aware of a presence greater than you, you will believe in God.

Example of the numinous

Father Yves Dubois has had numinous experiences while praying before a statue of the **Virgin Mary**.

'Twice I have experienced the presence of Mary, the Mother of God. It was an awareness of purity, holiness and love unlike anything I have ever known.'

Source: *Christians in Britain Today*, Hodder, 1991 (adapted)

Do you think Father Yves Dubois could doubt the existence of God after these numinous experiences?

2. Conversion and belief in God

'Conversion' is the word used to describe an experience of God, which is so great that the person experiencing it wants to change their life or religion and commit themselves to God in a special way.

'I don't try to imagine a personal God; but stand in awe at the structure of the world.'

Albert Einstein

Conversion experiences make people believe in God because they feel that God is calling them to do something for him.

Example of a conversion

Raymond Nader was a commander of a Christian militia group fighting against Muslim militias in the Lebanon Civil War. In November, he went to pray at St Charbel's chapel and felt surrounded by a great light which burned him when he tried to touch it. He felt it was St Charbel telling him to stop fighting. The experience made him leave the militia and found a Christian television station working for peace.

Do you think that Raymond Nader would have been able not to believe in God after this conversion experience?

Saul was on his way to Damascus to arrest the Christians there, when he had a vision of Jesus which blinded him. After this conversion experience, his sight recovered and he became a great Christian **missionary** and changed his name to Paul. This painting shows St Paul on the Road to Damascus. It was painted by Augustin Cranagh in 1560.

3. Miracles and belief in God

A miracle is an event that breaks a law of science and can only be explained by God.

Example of a miracle

This statue of the Hindu God Ganesh appeared to drink milk from a spoon.

In September 1995, milk was being offered to a statue of the Hindu god Ganesh in a temple in India, when the milk seemed to disappear. There was no sign of where it had gone. The worshippers offered the god milk on a spoon and at least half the spoonful of milk disappeared. This began to happen at other Hindu temples including those in Neasden, Wimbledon, Southall, Manchester and Leicester.

Miracles can lead to belief in God because, if a miracle has really happened, it means that God has acted on the earth, and so must exist. If you experience something that seems to break all the laws of science, you will look for an explanation. If the only explanation you can think of is a miracle, you will start believing in God.

Thousands of letters sent each year to God end up in a sorting office in Jerusalem. The letters arrive from all over the world in the city's undeliverable mail department. 'We have hundreds of thousands of letters sent to either God or Jesus Christ, and for some reason they all end up in Jerusalem,' said a post office spokesman, Yitzhak Rabihya. In one letter an Israeli man asked God for 5,000 shekels to ease his poverty. Postal workers were so moved that they sent him 4,300 shekels. 'After a month the same man wrote again to God,' Mr Rabiya explained, 'but this time he wrote, "Oh, thank you God for the contribution, but next time please don't send it through those postmen. They're thieves, they stole 700 shekels."'

Abridged from *The Times*, 4 October 2003

4. Prayer

Religious believers think they can make contact with God through prayer. Prayers may be made in worship (such as the Christian **Eucharist**, Muslim **Salah** or Hindu **arti**) or in private.

If the person praying feels that God is listening to the prayer, then they are likely to believe that God exists. Also, an answered prayer will lead to belief in God. An example of this is when someone prays for a sick loved one to recover and they do.

Example of prayer leading to belief

About ten years ago, I began to pray for my children's safety, and often my prayers have been answered so that I now feel I am in contact with God most of the time.

Source: Alister Hardy Trust, Oxford (adapted)

Any religious believer who has a religious experience will find that the experience makes their belief in God stronger. This is because they believe they have had direct contact with God.

George W. Bush's religious experiences led him to believe in God and change his life.

Exam focus

You must decide what you think about the issues and ideas you study. For this topic you should have thought about whether there is such a thing as the numinous and whether it means God exists; you should have thought about whether conversions really happen and whether they prove God exists; whether you believe in miracles and whether a miracle would prove that God exists; whether prayer is valuable. The questions are meant to be quite easy and to get full marks you just need to give two reasons.

Questions

b Do you think miracles prove that God exists? Give two reasons for your point of view. **4**

c Explain how religious experience can lead to, or support, belief in God. **8**

d 'Religious experiences prove that God exists.'
  i Do you agree? Give reasons for your opinion. **3**
  ii Give reasons why some people may disagree with you. **3**

Exam Tip

b You should already have thought about this, and you just have to give two reasons for your opinion. For example, if you think miracles prove God's existence, you could use these two reasons:
  - if a miracle happens there is no explanation for it except that God caused it to happen
  - Christians believe that Jesus rising from the dead proves he was God's Son because only God could rise from the dead.

SUMMARY

People claim to experience God in miracles, answered prayers, the numinous and conversion. Religious experience makes people feel that God is real.

Topic 1.3 The argument from design and belief in God

Could this car have been made without the design?

What is design?

Design means making a plan to produce something you want to produce. For example, a car is made to the plan of the car designer. Looking at any part of the car makes you think the car has been designed.

Evidence of design in the world

Laws of science

The way the universe works according to laws such as gravity and magnetism makes some people think it has been designed.

DNA

All living things are formed from DNA which is a nucleic acid.

The structure of DNA and the way it forms templates seem to be a blueprint for life on earth. A blueprint is another name for design, so DNA is evidence of design in the world.

Evolution

Some scientists also see evidence of design in the process of evolution where complex life forms develop from simple ones.

Beauty of nature

The beauties of nature (e.g. sunsets and mountains) seem to be designed.

Science, design and God

The question about the origins of the world and of man has been the object of many scientific studies that have splendidly enriched our knowledge ... These discoveries invite us to even greater admiration for the greatness of the Creator.

Catechism of the Catholic Church

If you came across a watch in a desert, you could not say it had been put there by chance. The complicated mechanism would make you say it had a designer. The universe is far more complicated than a watch, and so, if a watch needs a watchmaker, the universe needs a universe maker. And God is the only being that could design the universe.

Paley's Watch Argument for the Existence of God

How the appearance of design may lead to, or support, belief in God

This is often called the argument from design. It goes like this:

- Anything that has been designed needs a designer.
- There is plenty of evidence that the world has been designed (laws of science, DNA).
- If the world has been designed, the world must have a designer.
- The only possible designer of the world could be God.
- Therefore the appearance of design in the world proves that God exists.

This argument supports belief in God. It may also lead those who are not sure to believe in God.

How the appearance of design may not lead to belief in God

Many people think the argument from design does not prove God exists because:

- No designer would have created things like volcanoes, earthquakes, etc.
- Science can explain the appearance of design without needing God.
- The argument does not explain how things like dinosaurs could have been part of a design plan for the world.
- Even if the argument worked, it would only prove that the world has a designer. This may not be God.

Questions
b Do you think God designed the world? Give two reasons for your point of view. **4**
c Explain why the design argument leads some people to believe in God. **8**
d 'The design argument proves that God exists.'
  i Do you agree? Give reasons for your opinion. **3**
  ii Give reasons why some people may disagree with you. **3**

Topic 1.4 The argument from causation and belief in God

What is causation?

Causation is the process of one thing causing another. For example, in the diagram below, a driver pressing the brake pedal causes the the car to slow down.

Evidence of causation in the world

Cause and effect seem to be a basic feature of the world. Whatever we do has an effect. If I do my homework (cause), I will please my parents and/or teachers (effect). Modern science has developed through looking at causes and effects, especially looking for single causes of an effect (my parents' happiness may have been caused by other things than my doing my homework). Scientific investigations seem to show that any effect has a cause and any cause has an effect.

The argument from causation

The argument goes like this:

> If we look at things in the world, we see that they have a cause; for example, ice is caused by the temperature falling and water becoming solid at below 0°C.

> Anything caused to exist must be caused to exist by something else because to cause your own existence, you would have to exist before you exist, which is nonsense.

> You cannot keep going back with causes because in any causal chain you have to have a beginning; for example, you have to have water to produce ice.
> So if the universe has no First Cause, then there would be no universe, but as there is a universe, there must be a First Cause.

> The only possible First Cause of the universe is God, therefore God must exist.

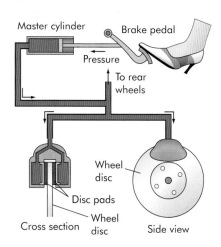

Putting your foot on the brake when driving a car causes pressure in the brake pipes, which causes the brake pads to put pressure on the discs, which causes the wheels to stop turning, which causes the car to slow down.

A good example of the argument is:

- In a long goods train, each wagon is caused to move by the wagon that is pulling it, which is caused to move by another wagon, etc.

10

- The goods train moving can only be explained if there is an engine which moves itself.
- In the same way, things in the universe being caused or moved by something else must have been started off by an Unmoved Mover. This could only be God.

Why some people disagree with the argument

Some people think the argument from causation does not work because:

- If everything needs a cause then God must need a cause.
- If matter is eternal (cannot be created or destroyed), the process of causes can go back for ever.
- Even if there was a First Cause it would not have to be God.

Does the universe need a First Cause? If so, and that First Cause is God, does God need a cause?

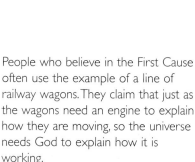

Behold! In the creation of the heavens and the earth ... Here indeed are signs for a people that are wise.

Surah 2:164

People who believe in the First Cause often use the example of a line of railway wagons. They claim that just as the wagons need an engine to explain how they are moving, so the universe needs God to explain how it is working.

Questions

b Do you think God is the cause of the universe? Give two reasons for your point of view. **4**

c Explain how the argument from causation may lead to belief in God. **8**

d 'The argument from causation proves that God exists.'
  i Do you agree? Give reasons for your opinion. **3**
  ii Give reasons why some people may disagree with you. **3**

Exam Tip

c To answer this question, you need to outline the argument and make sure you emphasise the conclusion (the last step in the flowchart) so that you show exactly how it might lead to belief in God. For tips on Quality of Written Communication, look at page 3.

SUMMARY

The way everything seems to have a cause makes people think the universe must have a cause, and the only possible cause of the universe is God, so God must exist.

Topic 1.5 Scientific explanations of the world and agnosticism and atheism

Science explains how the world came into being in this way:

- Matter is eternal. This means it cannot be created or destroyed, only changed.
- About 15 billion years ago, the matter of the universe exploded (the Big Bang).
- As the matter of the universe flew away from the explosion, it formed stars and then our solar system.
- The gases on the earth's surface produced primitive life forms.
- Changes in these life forms led to the evolution of new life forms and, about 2.5 million years ago, humans evolved.

Evidence for the Big Bang

The red shift in light from other galaxies is evidence that the universe is expanding (see photo below).

An alternative to the Big Bang?

Scientists from Princeton University claim that the universe began not with a Big Bang but a collision with another universe.

According to the scientists, a weak attraction brought two universes together, creating a collision that made particles and energy.

The scientists claim that the theory explains many observations of the universe better than the Big Bang.

Science Journal, April 2002

Evidence for evolution

The evidence of fossils shows new life forms coming into existence.

Genetic research shows the similarities of life forms (about 50 per cent of human DNA is the same as that of a cabbage).

How the scientific explanation of the world may lead to agnosticism or atheism

This Pterodactylus dinosaur fossil is over 145.5 million years old.

If science can explain the universe and humans without God, it can lead some people to be **agnostic**. This is because they no longer need God to explain why we are here.

Other people may become **atheists**. This is because they think the scientific explanation of the world and humans without God is proof that God does not exist.

Questions

b Do you agree with the scientific explanation of the world? Give two reasons for your point of view. **4**

c Explain why the scientific explanation of the world leads some people to become atheists or agnostics. **8**

d 'Science proves that God did not create the universe.'
  i Do you agree? Give reasons for your opinion. **3**
  ii Give reasons why some people may disagree with you. **3**

Exam Tip

d Use the answering evaluation questions advice from page 9. The arguments for the statement are in this topic, the arguments against are in Topic 1.6.

SUMMARY

Science says that matter is eternal and that the universe began when this matter exploded. The solar system came out of the explosion, and the nature of the earth allowed life to develop through evolution.

Topic 1.6 How one religion responds to scientific explanations of the world

Has all animal life come from the animals saved on Noah's ark?

There are three Christian responses to scientific explanations of the world.

Response one

Many Christians believe that the scientific explanations are true and prove that God created the universe because:

- Only God could have made the Big Bang at exactly the right micro second to form the universe.
- Only God could have made the laws like gravity which the matter of the Big Bang needed to form solar systems.
- Only God could have made the gases on earth react to form life.

Response two

Some Christians believe that all the evidence for the Big Bang and evolution can be explained by:

- the effects of Noah's flood
- the Apparent Age theory.

The Apparent Age theory claims that when Adam was made the earth was six days old, but to Adam it would have looked billions of years old because of the way God created it. So they believe science is wrong and the Bible is right. This response is known as **creationism**.

> *What is shown of the divine in the human life of Jesus is also to be seen in the story of creation.*
>
> J. Polkinghorne in *Science and Creation* (adapted)

Response three

Some Christians believe that both the scientific explanations and the Bible are correct. They claim that the main points of the Bible story fit with science, but one of God's days could be millions or billions of years.

Can we know how God created the world?

The point is that, for the existence of any forms of life... the necessary environment, whatever its nature, must be complex and dependent on many conditions, such as are not reasonably attributable to blind forces.

F. R. Tennant in *The Existence of God* (adapted)

Questions

b Do you think science shows that God did not design the world? Give two reasons for your point of view. **4**

c Choose one religion and explain how its followers respond to scientific explanations of the world. **8**

d 'The universe could only have been made by God.'
  i Do you agree? Give reasons for your opinion. **3**
  ii Give reasons why some people may disagree with you. **3**

Exam tip

c You must choose a religion so begin with the words 'In Christianity'. 'Explaining how' means explaining the responses of Christianity to the scientific explanation. You should take two responses and explain them in some detail to reach level 4. For tips on Quality of Written Communication, look at page 3.

SUMMARY

- Many Christians accept the scientific explanations but believe they show that God created the Universe through the Big Bang.
- Some Christians say the scientific explanations are wrong and the biblical story of creation is fact because it is the word of God.
- Some Christians believe that both science and the Bible are true because one of God's days could be billions of years.

Topic 1.7 How unanswered prayers may lead to agnosticism or atheism

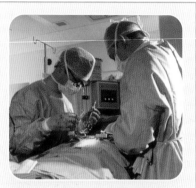

Prayer appears to have no effect on patients undergoing heart surgery, a new study has found. Researchers ... followed the progress of 750 patients, half of whom were prayed for by a team of Christians, Jews, Buddhists and Muslims. Those who were prayed for fared no better than those who were not.

The Times, 18 October 2003

If God exists, shouldn't those who pray have better results than those who do not?

As can be seen in Topic 1.2 Religious experience (pages 4–7), if people feel the presence of God and/or their prayers are answered they will believe in God. But if these do not happen, they may become agnostics or atheists.

Not feeling God's presence when praying

If people say their prayers in church and at home, but never feel the presence of God when they pray, they may feel there is no God listening to them. They may ask for advice and try even harder in their prayers. But if they still have no feeling of the presence of God when they pray, they will doubt that God is there at all. The feeling that no one is listening to their prayers leads them to agnosticism, or even atheism.

Prayers not being answered

Unanswered prayers are even more likely to lead people to believe God does not exist. Christians believe that God is their loving heavenly father who will answer their prayers, and they are often told about Christians whose prayers have been answered.

Example of an answered prayer

I spent five years with a boyfriend who would not commit himself to marriage. I was severely depressed and prayed to St Jude for help and now I am happily married.

However, if someone's prayers are not answered, they may begin to wonder why God answers some people's prayers, but not others.

This is very likely to happen if parents pray for their child to be cured of cancer, yet the child still dies. They may begin to think that God does not exist if he will let children die.

If their prayers continue to be unanswered, especially if they are praying for good things like the end of wars, or food for the starving, then they will stop believing in God. In this way, unanswered prayers can lead a person to become an agnostic or an atheist.

A young missionary couple asked the members of their church to pray that they would have a safe journey to their new posting in Nepal. However, the plane crashed killing them and their three young children.

Quoted in *If I were God I'd Say Sorry*

Why do you think the church's prayers were unanswered?

Questions

b Do you think unanswered prayers prove that God does not exist? Give two reasons for your point of view. **4**

c Explain why unanswered prayers may lead some people to become atheists. **8**

d 'God always answers prayers.'

   i Do you agree? Give reasons for your opinion. **3**

   ii Give reasons why some people may disagree with you. **3**

Exam Tip

d Use the evaluation technique on page 9. Evidence for God answering prayers is in Topic 1.8. Evidence against God answering prayers is in this topic.

SUMMARY

If people do not feel God's presence when they pray, or if people pray for good things, but their prayers are not answered, this might make some people doubt God's existence. If God does not answer prayers, how do you know he exists?

Topic 1.8 How one religion responds to unanswered prayers

Some even stop praying because they think their petition is not heard. Here two questions should be asked: Why do we think our petition has not been heard? How is our prayer heard, how is it efficacious?

Catechism of the Catholic Church 2734

Gracious Lord, oh bomb the Germans.
Spare their women for Thy Sake,
And if that is not too easy
We will pardon Thy Mistake,
But, gracious Lord, whate'er shall be,
Don't let anyone bomb me.

In Westminster Abbey, John Betjeman

Why do you think God might not have answered this prayer supposedly made by an Englishwoman during the Second World War?

Most Christians believe that God answers all prayers and that what seem to be unanswered prayers can be explained in different ways.

- If you pray for selfish things like God allowing you to pass an exam without any work, God will let you fail so that you work hard next time.
- Your prayer may not be answered in the way you expect because God has different plans. For example, he may want an ill person to enter heaven.
- Just like a human parent, God may answer our prayers by giving us what we need rather than what we have asked for.
- Christians believe that God loves people. They believe God's love will answer their prayers in the best possible way, even though it may not look like a direct answer.
- Christians have faith that God will answer all prayers in the best way for the person praying, or the people prayed for, even if it is different from what they expected.

Questions

b Do you think prayer is a waste of time? Give two reasons for your point of view. **4**

c Choose one religion and explain how its followers respond to unanswered prayers. **8**

d 'Unanswered prayers prove that God does not exist.'
  i Do you agree? Give reasons for your opinion. **3**
  ii Give reasons why some people may disagree with you. **3**

Exam tip

b You should already have thought about this, and you just have to give two reasons for your opinion. For example, if you think prayer is not a waste of time, you could use these two reasons:
  - For people who believe in God, prayer is the best way to improve their relationship with God.
  - If God answers your prayers, for example, by helping you pass an exam, you are not going to think prayer is waste of time.

SUMMARY

Christians believe that God cannot answer selfish prayers. But he answers all other prayers, though not always in the way people expect, because his answers have to fit in with his overall plans.

Topic 1.9 Evil and suffering

Evil and suffering can take two forms:

1. Moral evil

This is evil that is caused by humans using their **free will** (the human ability to make choices) to do something evil.

War is a good example of **moral evil**. Wars cause large amounts of suffering. All wars are caused by the actions of humans who could have chosen to act differently.

Rape, murder and burglary are clear examples of moral evil. People who commit these crimes choose to do evil and cause others suffering. Things like famines are less clear. If they are caused by landowners growing cash crops instead of food to make more money, they are moral evil. If they are caused by lack of rain they are not moral evil.

Christians often call moral evil sins because they are against what God wants humans to do. For example, they break the **Ten Commandments**.

2. Natural evil

Natural evil is suffering that has not been caused by humans. Earthquakes, floods, volcanoes, cancers and so on are not caused by humans, but they result in lots of human suffering.

> **KEY WORDS**
>
> Free will – the idea that human beings are free to make their own choices.
>
> Moral evil – actions done by humans which cause suffering.
>
> Natural evil – things which cause suffering but have nothing to do with humans.

> *You shall not murder.*
> *You shall not commit adultery.*
> *You shall not steal.*
> *You shall not give false testimony ...*
> *You shall not covet ...*
>
> The last five of the *Ten Commandments*, Exodus 20:13–17
>
> Would breaking these lead to moral evil?

The aftermath of the tsunami of December 2004 in Southeast Asia. This event caused many people to ask how God could let something like that happen.

KEY WORDS

Omni-benevolent – the belief that God is all-good.

Omnipotent – the belief that God is all-powerful.

Omniscient – the belief that God knows everything that has happened and everything that is going to happen.

How evil and suffering cause people to question or reject belief in God

How evil and suffering cause people to question or reject belief in God. Some people believe that a good God would not have designed a world with natural evils in it. If they had been God, they would not have created floods, earthquakes, volcanoes, cancers, etc. As God must be better than humans they cannot believe he would have created these things. So they believe natural evil shows God has not created the world.

Some people cannot believe in a God who allows humans to cause so much evil and suffering when he could stop it if he wanted to. As the suffering was not stopped, this may mean that God does not exist.

> I cannot imagine any omnipotent being cruel enough to create the world we inhabit.
>
> *The Severed Head*, Murdoch (adapted)

A mother crying after her home has been destroyed by an earthquake. Would a good omnipotent God cause so much suffering?

> How are atheists produced? In probably nine cases out of ten, what happens is something like this:
>
> *A beloved husband, or wife, or child, or sweetheart is gnawed to death by cancer ... and the looker-on, after praying vainly to God to stop such horrible cruelty, stops believing in the divine monster.*
>
> *St Joan*, George Bernard Shaw (1856–1950) (adapted)

Philosophers express the problem in this way:

- If God is **omnipotent** (all-powerful), he must be able to remove evil and suffering from the world.
- If God is **omni-benevolent** (all-good), he must want to remove evil and suffering from the world
- It follows that, if God exists, there should be no evil or suffering in the world.
- As there is evil and suffering in the world, either God is not all-good and powerful or he does not exist.

Also, if God knows everything (**omniscient**), he must have known the evil and suffering that would come from creating the universe. So he should have created the universe in a way that avoided evil and suffering.

Most religious believers believe that God is omnipotent, omni-benevolent and omniscient. So the existence of evil and suffering challenges their beliefs about God.

For many religious believers evil and suffering become a problem if they experience it (e.g. they are in an earthquake, or their child dies from a disease). This may change them into an atheist or agnostic.

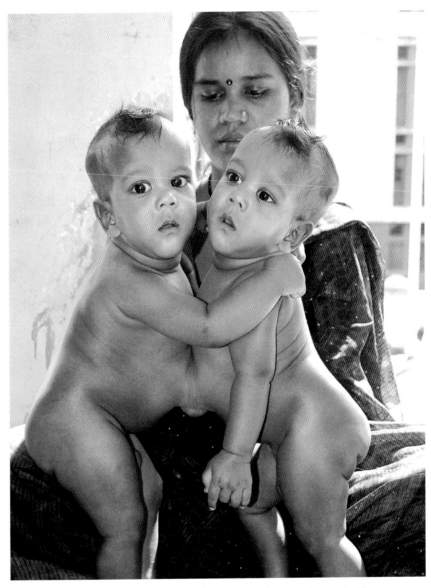

Should there be the sufferings of conjoined twins in a world created by an omnipotent and omni-benevolent God?

Questions

b Do you think evil and suffering show that God does not exist? Give two reasons for your point of view. **4**

c Explain how the existence of evil and suffering may lead some people to deny God's existence. **8**

d 'A loving God would not let us suffer.'
   i Do you agree? Give reasons for your opinion. **3**
   ii Give reasons why some people may disagree with you. **3**

Exam Tip

c Look at the problems caused to people's lives by evil and suffering and explain why these may stop them believing in God – remember to include the philosophers' explanation. For tips on Quality of Written Communication, look at page 3.

SUMMARY

Some people do not believe in God because they think that there would be no evil and suffering in a world created by a good and powerful God. A good God should not want such things to happen, and a powerful God ought to be able to get rid of them but does not.

Topic 1.10 How one religion responds to the problem of evil and suffering

There are several Christian responses to the problem of evil and suffering. Most Christians would use at least two to explain how an all-good, all-powerful God can allow evil and suffering.

Then the righteous will answer him, 'Lord, when did we see you hungry and feed you, or thirsty and give you something to drink? When did we see you a stranger and invite you in, or needing clothes and clothe you? When did we see you sick or in prison and go to visit you?' The King will reply, 'I tell you the truth, whatever you did for one of the least of these brothers of mine, you did for me.'

Matthew 25:37–40

Response one

Christians believe that God wants them to help those who suffer. The **New Testament** teaches Christians that Jesus fought evil and suffering by:

- healing the sick
- feeding the hungry
- challenging those who were evil
- raising the dead.

Many Christians believe from the Bible that God must have a reason for allowing evil and suffering. They believe humans cannot understand this reason. Therefore, the correct response of Christians is to follow the example of Jesus and fight against evil and suffering.

Christians do this by:

- Praying for those who suffer. All Christian services include prayers asking God to help those who suffer from poverty, sickness, famine, war, and so on. Christians believe that prayer is a powerful way of dealing with a problem.

A CAFOD (Catholic Agency for Overseas Development) partner with armed child soldiers. Do you think Christians feel they need to do this kind of work because of the words of Jesus in Matthew 25?

- By helping those who suffer. Many Christians become doctors, nurses and social workers, for example, so that they can help to reduce the amount of suffering in the world.

Response two

Many Christians claim that, by making humans with free will, God created a world in which evil and suffering will come about through humans misusing their free will. So evil and suffering are a problem caused by humans, not God.

'The Children's Society helped me get my life back after I ran away from home and started taking drugs – I don't know what I would have done without them.'

Response three

Many Christians believe that the evil and suffering involved in this life are not a problem because this life is a preparation for paradise. If people are to improve their souls they need to face evil and suffering in order to become good, kind and loving. God cannot remove evil and suffering if he is going to give people the chance to become good people. But, in the end, he will show his omni-benevolence and omnipotence by rewarding the good in heaven.

Response four

Some Christians claim that God has a reason for not using his power to remove evil and suffering, but humans cannot understand it. God is divine and there is no way humans can understand his thoughts.

While God cannot be said to be responsible for the world's evil, he has assumed responsibility for it by creating a world such as ours in the first place. That is to say, he is not a distant God, but somehow present in the evil, loving and suffering with those who suffer it, and enabling people to triumph over it by bringing good out of evil.

Private Notes, Peter de Rosa, a twentieth–century Christian thinker

God is in the cancer as he is in the sunset, and is to be met and responded to in each. Both are faces of God, the one terrible, the other beautiful … The problem of evil is not how God can will it, but its power to threaten meaninglessness and separation

Exploration into God, J. A. T. Robinson, a twentieth–century Christian thinker SCM 1967

Questions

b Do you think God allows us to suffer? Give two reasons for your point of view. **4**

c Choose one religion and explain how its followers respond to the problem of evil and suffering. **8**

d 'Evil and suffering in the world prove that God does not exist.'
  i Do you agree? Give reasons for your opinion. **3**
  ii Give reasons why some people may disagree with you. **3**

Exam Tip

d Use the evaluation technique on page 9. Evidence for evil and suffering proving God does not exist is in Topic 1.9. Evidence against evil and suffering proving God does not exist is in this topic.

SUMMARY

Christians respond to the problem of evil and suffering by:
- praying for those who suffer
- helping those who suffer
- claiming that evil and suffering are the fault of humans misusing their free will
- claiming that evil and suffering are part of a test to prepare people for heaven.

Topic 1.11 How two programmes about religion could affect a person's attitude to belief in God

Study two religious programmes/films and work out how they could affect a person's attitude to belief in God.

Why do you think *The Convent* reality show became so popular?

The programmes do not have to be factual programmes about religion (for example, *Songs of Praise, The Convent, A Seaside Parish, The Miracles of Jesus*). The important thing is that they should be about belief in God, so programmes like *The Simpsons* and *The Vicar of Dibley* or films like *Bruce Almighty* could be used as long as they have enough content about belief in God.

When you have chosen your two programmes/films, you need to:

1 Write a summary of the programme.

2 Decide which parts of the programme might have encouraged some people to believe in God. Write down four pieces of evidence from the programme for this.

3 Decide which parts of the programme might have encouraged some people not to believe in God. Write down four pieces of evidence from the programme for this.

4 Decide what effect the programme had on your own attitude to belief in God. Write down four reasons for this.

> *Where have we come from?*
>
> *Why are we here?*
>
> *How should we live?*
>
> *BBC Religion exists to ask the big questions that underlie all human life and explore the different ways in which people try to answer them, whether through worship, prayer, or simply giving food for thought.*
>
> **The aim of Religious Broadcasting by the BBC**

24

Sample programme – *Songs of Praise*

On Sunday 3 February 2008, *Songs of Praise* came from St Wilfred's, Harrogate. Two of the interviews and the hymns might have affected belief in God.

Mark Pallant, Head of Music at St Aidan's Church of England High School, talked about his own faith, and how he feels that music can put people in touch with God. If you had watched this programme, you would need to note the points Mark made and decide which ones would encourage some people to believe in God and which ones would not. Then you would need to decide whether it affected your beliefs in God and why it did or did not.

Phil Willis, the MP for Harrogate, talked about how he changed from an agnostic to a Christian. You would need to note the points Phil made and decide which ones would encourage some people to believe in God and which ones would not. Then you would need to decide whether it affected your beliefs in God and why it did or did not.

You would need to watch the singing of the hymns, listen to the music and think about the words to gain evidence about whether or not they would influence people's attitudes (including your own) to belief in God.

Phil Willis, the Liberal Democrat MP for Harrogate.

Sample programme – *The Sunday Edition*

On 27 December 2006, *The Sunday Edition* featured a discussion between Tony Benn, a Christian agnostic politician, and Richard Dawkins, an atheist scientist, and author of *The God Delusion*.

If you watched this programme, you would need to note what things were said that might make people disbelieve in God, and what things were said that might make people believe in God. You would then need to decide what you thought and why.

Sample programme – *Only Fools and Horses*

In the episode 'The Miracle of Peckham', this classic BBC sitcom investigated the nature of miracles in a very amusing way.

It begins with Del Boy going to church to confess his **sin** of handling stolen goods. The priest begins to voice his doubts about God's existence, because the church hospice is being closed down unless they can raise £1 million. As Del Boy leaves the church the statue of the Virgin Mary starts crying. By selling the TV and newspaper rights to the miracle they raise the money for the hospice. However, the 'miracle' tears were really drops of rain as the lead had been stolen from the roof.

If you had watched this programme, you would need to note what happened and what was said that might encourage people to believe in God. You would then need to note what happened and what was said that might encourage some people not to believe in God. Finally, you would need to decide how the programme affected your beliefs about God.

A Seaside Parish was a fly-on-the-wall documentary about the work of a divorced, re-married woman priest, Reverend Christine Musser. She was the new vicar of Boscastle, a village in Cornwall. It proved surprisingly popular and is now into its third series.

Questions

b Do you think programmes about religion can affect your belief in God? Give two reasons for your point of view. **4**

c Choose one programme about religion and explain how it might affect someone's belief about God. **8**

d 'Religious programmes on television or the radio encourage you to believe in God.'

　i Do you agree? Give reasons for your opinion. **3**

　ii Give reasons why some people may disagree with you. **3**

Exam Tip

d Use the evaluation technique on page 9. Evidence for your own opinion will come from your notes about how the programme affected your attitude to belief in God. Evidence for why some people might disagree with you will come from your notes on the programme either on how it encouraged or how it discouraged belief in God.

SUMMARY

You need to study two programmes about religion. For each one you will need to know:

● an outline of its contents

● how it might have encouraged some people to believe in God

● how it might have encouraged some people not to believe in God

● whether it affected your beliefs about God.

How to answer exam questions

Question A What is atheism? 2 marks

Atheism is believing that there is no God.

Question B Do you think God is the cause of the universe?
Give two reasons for your point of view. 4 marks

Yes I do think that God is the cause of the universe because everything needs a cause and God is the only thing that could have created something as big as the universe. Also I am a Christian and it is one of the beliefs of Christianity that God created the universe. In fact it says so in the creed.

Question C Explain how a religious upbringing can lead to, or support, belief in God. 8 marks

Christians usually teach their children to pray to God. This will make the children believe that God exists because otherwise their parents would not want them to pray to him. If God did not exist, they and their parents would not waste their time praying to nothing. Also they may feel God's presence when they pray. So because they've been brought up to pray, they believe that God must exist.

Another feature of a Christian upbringing is going to church. When children go to church they see lots of people praying to God and worshipping God and this is bound to make them think that God must exist because all these people believe he does.

Many Christian parents also send their children to a Church school. Here they will have RE lessons which teach them that God exists and the children are likely to believe it because their teachers tell them it is true.

Question D 'Considering the evidence, everyone should be an agnostic.'

i Do you agree? Give reasons for your opinion. 3 marks

ii Give reasons why some people may disagree with you. 3 marks

i I do not agree because I am an atheist, not an agnostic. I think that science, the Big Bang, DNA and evolution are compelling proof that God does not exist because he did not create the universe or people. Also if God existed, surely he would have sent only one holy book, he would allow only one religion. Furthermore, the fact of evil and suffering in the world proves that God does not exist, because an all-good and all-powerful being would not allow it. The evidence of science, the problem of evil and suffering, and the huge problems of different religions convince me that there is no God and so I disagree with the statement.

ii I can see why some people would disagree with me because evidence such as design can be used both for and against God's existence. The Design Argument seems to prove God's existence, but the Big Bang seems to disprove it. In the same way the First Cause argument seems to prove God's existence, but then there is the question of what caused God. Then the religious evidence to prove God's existence such as miracles, holy books, etc., can be explained in non-religious ways. So, it seems logical to say there is not enough evidence either way, so some people are agnostics.

QUESTION A
High marks because it is a correct definition.

QUESTION B
A high mark answer because an opinion is backed up by two developed reasons.

QUESTION C
A high mark answer because it begins with a developed reason on how being taught to pray leads to belief in God. This is backed up by two further reasons – going to worship and going to a church school. It is written in a formal style of English in sentences and paragraphs. The spelling is good and it uses specialist vocabulary such as prayer, worship, church, God's presence.

QUESTION D
A high mark answer because it states the candidate's own opinion and backs it up with three clear reasons for thinking that the evidence for atheism is greater than the evidence for agnosticism. It then gives three reasons for people disagreeing and believing that the evidence shows that everyone should be agnostic.

Section 2 **Matters of life and death**

Introduction

This section of the examination specification requires you to look at issues surrounding life after death, abortion, euthanasia, and the media and matters of life and death.

Life after death
You will need to understand the effects of, and give reasons for your own opinion about:
- why Christians believe in life after death and how this belief affects their lives
- why the followers of one religion other than Christianity believe in life after death and how this belief affects their lives
- non-religious reasons for believing in life after death (near-death experiences, ghosts, mediums, the evidence of reincarnation)
- why some people do not believe in life after death.

Abortion
You will need to understand the effects of, and give reasons for your own opinion about:
- the nature of abortion, including current UK legislation, and non-religious arguments about abortion
- different Christian attitudes to abortion and the reasons for them
- different attitudes to abortion in one religion other than Christianity and the reasons for them.

Euthanasia
You will need to understand the effects of, and give reasons for your own opinion about:
- the nature of euthanasia including current British legislation, and non-religious arguments about euthanasia
- different Christian attitudes to euthanasia and the reasons for them
- different attitudes to euthanasia in one religion other than Christianity and the reasons for them.

The media and matters of life and death
You will need to understand the effects of, and give reasons for your own opinion about arguments over whether the media should or should not be free to criticise religious attitudes to matters of life and death.

Topic 2.1 Christian beliefs about life after death

KEY WORDS

Immortality of the soul – the idea that the soul lives on after the death of the body.

Paranormal – unexplained things which are thought to have spiritual causes, for example, ghosts, mediums.

Resurrection – the belief that, after death, the body stays in the grave until the end of the world, when it is raised.

Why Christians believe in life after death

Christians believe that this life is not all there is. They believe God will reward the good and punish the bad in some form of life after death.

All Christians believe in life after death because:

- The main Christian belief is that Jesus rose from the dead. All four **Gospels** record the death and **resurrection** of Jesus. The rest of the New Testament is full of references to the resurrection of Jesus. This proves there is life after death.
- **St Paul** teaches that people will have a resurrection like that of Jesus.
- The major **creeds** of the Church teach that Jesus rose from the dead and that there will be life after death. Christians are supposed to believe the creeds and so they should believe in life after death.
- All the Christian Churches teach that there is life after death. **Protestant**, Catholic, **Orthodox** and **Pentecostal** Churches may have some differences about what they think life after death will be like, but they all teach their followers that there will be life after death.
- Many Christians believe that people are made up of a body and a soul and that the soul is non-material and immortal (will never die). They believe the soul lives on in heaven after the death of the body.

For what I received I passed on to you as of first importance: that Christ died for our sins according to the Scriptures, that he was buried, that he was raised on the third day according to the Scriptures and that he appeared to Peter, and then to the Twelve ... But if it is preached that Christ has been raised from the dead, how can some of you say that there is no resurrection of the dead ... For as in Adam all die, so in Christ all will be made alive.

1 Corinthians 15: 3–5, 12, 22

I believe in ...
the resurrection of the body
and the life everlasting.

Apostles' Creed

- Many Christians believe in life after death because it gives their lives meaning and purpose. They feel that a life after death, in which people will be judged on how they live this life with the good rewarded and the evil punished, makes sense of this life.
- Some Christians believe in life after death because of the evidence of the **paranormal** (see Topic 2.3, page 42).

Some Christians believe that the tunnel of light seen in near-death experiences is evidence that heaven exists. Do you agree?

Jesus links faith in the resurrection to his own person: 'I am the Resurrection and the life.' It is Jesus himself who on the Last Day will raise up those who have believed in him.

Catechism of the Catholic Church 994

'I think, therefore I am.'

This famous statement by the philosopher Descartes is used by some Christians to show that the mind is separate from, and greater than, the body. They claim this means the mind can live without the body, and so they believe in the **immortality of the soul**.

How Christian beliefs about life after death affect the lives of Christians

1 Christians believe that what happens to them after they die will be based on how they have lived this life.

   This means that Christians will try to live a good Christian life following the teachings of the Bible and the Church so that they go to heaven when they die.

2 Living a good Christian life means loving God and loving your neighbour as yourself. So Christians' lives will be affected as they try to love God by praying every day and by worshipping God every Sunday.

3 Trying to love your neighbour as yourself is bound to affect a Christian's life. In the parable of the Sheep and Goats Jesus said Christians should:

   • feed the hungry
   • clothe the naked
   • befriend strangers
   • visit the sick and those in prison.

   Jesus taught in the Good Samaritan that loving your neighbour means helping anyone in need. These teachings are bound to affect Christians' lives and explain why Christians work for Christian Aid, CAFOD, etc.

4 Christians believe that sin can prevent people from going to heaven. Indeed some Christians believe that those who die with unforgiven sins will go to hell. These beliefs mean that Christians will try to avoid committing sins in their lives so that they will go to heaven.

The Parable of the Good Samaritan

'Which of these three do you think was a neighbour to the man who fell into the hands of robbers?' The expert in the law replied, 'The one who had mercy on him.'

Luke 10:36–37

Every action of yours, every thought, should be those of one who expects to die before the day is out. Death would have no terrors for you if you had a quiet conscience.

The Imitation of Christ by Thomas à Kempis (a medieval saint)

5 Christian beliefs about life after death give Christians' lives meaning and purpose. This may be why, in surveys, Christians suffer less from depression than atheists and agnostics.

How does a necropolis (city of the dead), like this one in Glasgow, show Christian belief in life after death?

Questions

b Do you think Christians are right to believe in life after death? Give two reasons for your point of view. **4**

c Explain why Christians believe in life after death. **8**

d 'Christians only believe in life after death because they're scared of dying.'
  i Do you agree? Give reasons for your opinion. **3**
  ii Give reasons why some people may disagree with you. **3**

Exam Tip

c 'Explain' means give reasons. To answer this question you should use four reasons from this section, and make each of them into a short paragraph. For tips on Quality of Written Communication, look at page 3.

SUMMARY

Christians believe in life after death because:
- Jesus rose from the dead
- the Bible and the Creeds say there is life after death
- the Church teaches that there is life after death
- the soul is something that can never die.

Their beliefs about life after death affect their lives because Christians will try to love God and love their neighbour so that they go to heaven and not hell.

Topic 2.2.1 Islam and life after death

> *That Day shall all men be sorted out. Then those who have believed and worked righteous deeds shall be made happy in a mead of delight. And those who have rejected faith and falsely denied Our signs and the meeting of the Hereafter, such shall be brought to punishment.*
>
> **Qur'an 30:14–16**

Why Muslims believe in life after death

Muslims believe in life after death because:

- The **Qur'an** teaches that there is life after death. Muslims believe that the Qur'an is the word of God and so its teachings must be true.
- Muhammad taught that there is life after death. Muslims believe that the **Prophet Muhammad** is the last prophet and the perfect example so his teachings must be true.
- Belief in life after death is a major part of the six beliefs of Islam which all Muslims are expected to believe. So Muslims must believe in life after death.
- Muslims believe that this life is a test from God which must involve a judgement as to how they have done in the test, with rewards for those who pass. This can only happen if there is life after death.
- Many Muslims believe in life after death because it gives their lives meaning and purpose. They feel that for life to end at death does not make sense. Living your life in such a way that you spend eternity in heaven gives life meaning.

> *And fear the Day when ye shall be brought back to God. Then shall every soul be paid what it earned, and none shall be dealt with unjustly.*
>
> **Qur'an 2:281**

Because of their beliefs about life after death, Muslims are never cremated. They are buried (facing **Makkah**) as soon as possible with no organs removed from the body.

How Muslim beliefs about life after death affect the lives of Muslims

1 Islam teaches that on the Last Day, all humans will be judged by God. Those who have lived good Muslim lives will go to paradise, everyone else will go to hell. This affects Muslims' lives because they must try to live good Muslim lives to avoid hell.

2 Living a good Muslim life means keeping the **Five Pillars** of Islam (praying five times a day, fasting during **Ramadan**, paying **zakah**, going on **hajj**). So their beliefs about life after death will have a big effect on their lives.

3 Living a good Muslim life also means following the holy law of Islam, the **Shari'ah**. This means eating **halal** food, observing Muslim dress laws, not drinking alcohol, not gambling or being involved in lending money to receive interest, etc.

4 Muslims believe that resurrection means that nothing should be removed from the body after death. This affects Muslim lives because they try to avoid post-mortems and many Muslims have concerns about transplant surgery.

5 Muslim beliefs about life after death give their lives meaning and purpose. This may be why, in surveys, Muslims suffer less from depression than atheists and agnostics.

Muslims prepare for the Last Day when they confess their sins at **Arafat**.

Let him who believes in Allah and the Last Day either speak good or keep silent, and let him who believes in Allah and the Last Day be generous to his neighbour, and let him who believes in Allah and the Last Day be generous to his guest.

Hadith recorded by al'Bukhari and Muslim

Questions

b Do you believe in life after death? Give two reasons for your point of view. **4**

c Choose one religion other than Christianity and explain how its beliefs about life after death affect the lives of its followers. **8**

d 'Your soul will never die.'
   i Do you agree? Give reasons for your opinion. **3**
   ii Give reasons why some people may disagree with you. **3**

Exam Tip

c Remember to say which religion you have chosen. 'Explain' means give reasons. To answer this question you should name four Muslim beliefs about life after death and explain, in two or three sentences for each, how they might affect a Muslim's life. For tips on Quality of Written Communication, look at page 3.

SUMMARY

Muslims believe in life after death because it is taught in the Qur'an, in the hadith of the Prophet and is one of the essential six beliefs of Islam.

Their beliefs about life after death affect their lives because Muslims will try to follow the Five Pillars and the teachings of the Shari'ah so that they go to heaven and not hell.

Topic 2.2.2 Judaism and life after death

Why Jewish people believe in life after death

Jewish people believe in life after death because:

- It is the teaching of the **Tenakh** which is inspired by God. Therefore Jews should believe what the Tenakh says.
- It is the teaching of the **Talmud** which most Jews try to follow because it is the teaching of **rabbis**.
- It is one of the **Thirteen Principles of Faith** which is part of the Jewish creed, and so should be believed.
- Many Jews believe in life after death because it gives their lives meaning and purpose. A life after death, in which people will be judged on how they live this life with the good rewarded and the evil punished, makes sense of this life.
- Some Jews believe in life after death because of the evidence of the paranormal (see Topic 2.3, page 42).

How Jewish beliefs about life after death affect the lives of Jewish people

1   Most Jews believe that God will decide what happens to people after they die on the basis of how they have lived their lives. This affects the lives of Jewish people because they must try to live good Jewish lives if they are to have a good life after death.

2   Living a good Jewish life means:

- observing the **Torah** and **halakhah**
- praying three times a day
- fasting on **Yom Kippur**
- keeping **Shabbat**
- celebrating the many festivals.

Therefore their beliefs about life after death will have a big effect on their lives.

3 Living a good Jewish life also means following all the **mitzvot**, keeping **kosher**, observing the dress laws, and not being involved in lending money to receive interest, etc.

4 **Orthodox Jews** believe that they should confess their sins before they die, help with funerals and keep shiva. This affects their lives because they are always aware of death.

5 Jewish beliefs about life after death give their lives meaning and purpose. This may be why, in surveys, Jewish people suffer less from depression than atheists and agnostics.

A Jewish cemetery at Southgate, London. Why is this called the House of Life?

> In the last days the mountain of the Lord's temple will be established as chief among the mountains; it will be raised above the hills, and all nations will stream to it.
>
> **Isaiah 2:2**

Questions

b Do you believe in life after death? Give two reasons for your point of view. **4**

c Choose one religion other than Christianity and explain how its beliefs about life after death affect the lives of its followers. **8**

d 'Your soul will never die.'
  i Do you agree? Give reasons for your opinion. **3**
  ii Give reasons why some people may disagree with you. **3**

Exam Tip

c Remember to say which religion you have chosen. 'Explain' means give reasons. To answer this question you should name four Jewish beliefs about life after death and explain, in two or three sentences for each, how they might affect a Jew's life. For tips on Quality of Written Communication, look at page 3.

SUMMARY

Jewish people believe in life after death because it is the teaching of the Tenakh and Talmud, and is one of the Thirteen Principles of Faith.

Their beliefs about life after death affect their lives because Orthodox Jews will try to follow the halakhah so that they go to heaven and not hell.

Topic 2.2.3 Hinduism and life after death

Why Hindus believe in life after death

Hindus believe in life after death because:

- It is taught in the **Vedas**, which contain eternal truths that most Hindus believe.
- It is taught in the **Upanishads**, which many Hindus also believe to contain eternal truths.
- It is taught in the **Bhagavad Gita**, and most Hindus feel that the teachings of the Gita contain ultimate truths and so must be believed.
- Many Hindus feel that for life to end at death does not make sense. **Reincarnation** rewards the good and punishes the evil when they die, which makes sense of this life.
- Hindus also believe in life after death because of the evidence for reincarnation, for example children who are born knowing things they could not know unless they had been on earth before.

What a man becomes in his next life depends upon his **karma**. *By good deeds he attains merit, by bad actions he becomes evil. The karma of a man ruled by desire attaches to his* **atman***, so that he is forced to suffer rebirth and return to the world of men. When all attachment arising from desire is destroyed, man's mortality ends and only then does atman reach Brahman.*

Upanishads IV.4:3–5

The Gita records that in his meeting with Krishna, the soldier, Arjuna, learned about the nature of the soul and rebirth.

How Hindu beliefs about life after death affect the lives of Hindus

1   The aim of Hindu life is to: escape from keep being reborn (**samsara**) through reaching **moksha** (freedom from rebirth) when the soul lives in paradise often called **nirvana**.

This affects the lives of Hindus because they must try to live the type of life that will lead them to moksha.

2   The lives of some Hindus are very affected because they follow all the rules of the four stages of life (**ashrama**) in order to reach moksha.

3   These Hindus believe in the **law of karma** and so they only do things in this life that will bring good effects in their next life.

4   Some Hindus believe that the way to gain moksha is by devotion to **Krishna**, and spend a lot of time in worship (**puja**) both at home and in the **mandir**.

5   Some Hindus believe that moksha is achieved through deep meditation to achieve oneness with **Brahman** (jnana yoga). This has a huge effect on their lives as they live alone to spend sufficient time in meditation.

As a man casts off his worn out clothes and takes on other new ones in their place, so does the embodied soul cast off his worn out bodies and enters others anew ... For sure is the death of all that comes to birth, sure the birth of all that dies.

Bhagavad Gita 2:18, 22, 27

A Hindu cremation on the banks of the River Ganges in India. Why are Hindus cremated?

Questions

b   Do you believe in life after death? Give two reasons for your point of view.   **4**

c   Choose one religion other than Christianity and explain how its beliefs about life after death affect the lives of its followers.   **8**

d   'Your soul will never die.'
    i   Do you agree? Give reasons for your opinion.   **3**
    ii Give reasons why some people may disagree with you.   **3**

Exam Tip

c   Remember to say which religion you have chosen. 'Explain' means give reasons. To answer this question you should name four Hindu beliefs about life after death and explain, in two or three sentences for each, how they might affect a Hindu's life. For tips on Quality of Written Communication, look at page 3.

SUMMARY

Hindus believe in life after death because it is the teaching of the Vedas, Upanishads and Gita. Their beliefs about life after death affect their lives because they will try to gain moksha either by living a good life, or living a life devoted to God or by living a life of meditation.

Topic 2.2.4 Sikhism and life after death

Know the real purpose of being here, gather up treasure under the True Guru's guidance. Make your mind God's home. If God abides with you undisturbed, you will not be reborn.

Guru Granth Sahib 13

Humanity is brimful of the nectar of God's name. Through tasting it, its relish is known. Those who taste it become free from fear and find that God's elixir satisfies their needs. Whoever is made to drink it through divine grace is never again afflicted by death.

Guru Granth Sahib 1092

Why Sikhs believe in life after death

Sikhs believe in life after death because:

- It is taught in the **Guru Granth Sahib** which Sikhs regard as their living Guru and so must be believed. Many Sikhs regard the Guru Granth Sahib as the words of God.
- The **Ten Gurus** all believed in life after death. Sikhs should follow both the examples and the teachings of the human Gurus, and so should believe in life after death.
- Sikhs believe that God would not have created humans without a purpose. A good God is bound to have created a life after death for his creatures.
- Many Sikhs feel that for life to end at death does not make sense. Reincarnation rewards the good and punishes the evil when they die, which makes sense of this life.
- Sikhs also believe in life after death because of the evidence for reincarnation. For example, children born knowing things they could not know unless they had been on earth before.

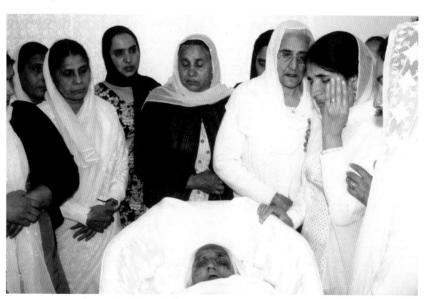

The Sikh funeral service says, 'The dawn of a new day is the herald of a sunset. Earth is not your permanent home.'
Guru Granth Sahib 793

How Sikh beliefs about life after death affect the lives of Sikhs

Sikhism teaches that souls are reborn (**samsara**) until pure enough to reach **mukti** (release from rebirth).

The way to mukti is to move from being human centred (**manmukh**) to being God-centred (**gurmukh**) and enter paradise.

This is bound to affect a Sikh's life as they try to follow the Gurus' teachings on how to reach paradise.

How does the way the Guru Granth Sahib is being treated show that Sikhs should believe what their holy book says about life after death?

Questions

b Do you believe in life after death? Give two reasons for your point of view. **4**

c Choose one religion other than Christianity and explain how its beliefs about life after death affect the lives of its followers. **8**

d 'Your soul will never die.'
   i Do you agree? Give reasons for your opinion. **3**
   ii Give reasons why some people may disagree with you. **3**

Exam Tip

c Remember to say which religion you have chosen. 'Explain' means give reasons. To answer this question you should name four Sikh beliefs about life after death and explain, in two or three sentences for each, how they might affect a Sikh's life. For tips on Quality of Written Communication, look at page 3.

SUMMARY

Sikhs believe in life after death because it is the teaching of the Guru Granth Sahib and the Ten Gurus.

Their beliefs about life after death affect their lives because they will try to gain mukti by living a good life which is God-centred.

Topic 2.3 Non-religious reasons for believing in life after death

Non-religious reasons for believing in life after death are connected to the paranormal (see page 30). There are three main parts of the paranormal that provide reasons for believing in life after death:

1. Near-death experiences

Near-death experiences are when someone is clinically dead for a time and then comes back to life, and can remember what happened. Research by doctors in Britain, Holland and the USA has shown that about eight per cent of patients who survived a heart attack had a near-death experience.

The main features of these experiences are:

- feelings of peace
- floating above the body
- seeing a bright light
- entering a heavenly place where they see dead relatives.

Example

Jeanette Mitchell-Meadows was having an operation when she felt herself leave her body. She followed a bright light to a place that felt like heaven where she met Jesus and her dead daughter and grandparents. She was told God still had things for her to do and she returned to her body.

If near-death experiences are true, there must be life after death.

2. Evidence for a spirit world

Many people think of ghosts and ouija boards as evidence for a spirit world, but the clearest evidence comes from mediums.

A medium is a person who claims to be able to communicate between our material world and a spirit world where the spirits of the dead live.

This research is very good work, which is needed to understand the near-death experience, but it proves absolutely nothing about the soul. All claims about this being evidence for consciousness existing without a brain are unfounded, baseless rubbish.

Dr Sue Blackmore

We are quite good at knowing that something happened, but we are very poor at knowing when it happened. It is quite possible that these experiences happened during the recovery or just before the cardiac arrest. To say that they happened when the brain was shut down, I think there is little evidence for that at all.

Dr Chris Freeman, Consultant Psychiatrist

There are mediums in all countries and in all religions. They feature frequently on television channels such as Living TV.

There are many TV shows featuring mediums. Two of the most famous are Craig and Jane Hamilton-Parker, who claim they met through Craig contacting the spirit of Jane's dead grandmother.

Most mediums claim that religious leaders like Jesus and Muhammad were in touch with the spirit world, so their religions do not have the only truth. They claim the spirit world gives people a second chance at life.

Mediums contact people's dead relatives giving information they would not be able to without their contact being true.

Example of evidence for spirit world

The medium Stephen O'Brien told a woman that he could see a peasant Mexican grandmother who wanted to thank the woman for helping her grandson. He said the word Cruz was coming to him. The woman was amazed because she was sponsoring a young Mexican boy whose surname was Cruz.

If mediums can contact the dead, there must be life after death.

Robert Thouless (President of the Society for Psychical Research) made an encrypted message before he died that would allow mediums to prove that they had contacted him after his death. At least 100 mediums submitted keys to the cypher, but none were correct, whereas a computer program solved it easily. A simple explanation is that Thouless had not survived death and so could not be contacted by mediums.

The Case Against Immortality by Keith Augustine (adapted)

The theory that mediums communicate with discarnate intelligences becomes even more suspect in the light of experiments in which mediumistic contact has been made with living or demonstrably fictional characters.

From *Paranormal Experiences and Survival of Death* by C. Becker

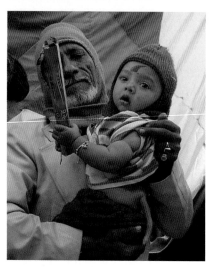

Baby with tail who some Hindus believe to be a reincarnation of a Hindu god.

> *In only eleven of the approximate 1,111 rebirth cases had there been no contact between the two families before an investigation was begun. Of these, seven were seriously flawed in some respect ... The rebirth cases are anecdotal evidence of the weakest sort.*
>
> **From *Immortality* by Paul Edwards**

3. The evidence of reincarnation

Hindus, Sikhs and Buddhists believe in reincarnation and have collected much evidence for this happening.

Example of reincarnation

In 1996 Taranjit Singh was born to a poor peasant family and received no education. He claimed, from the age of two, to have had a previous life. He was taken to the village he said he came from where his account of his death was confirmed. He could also write in English and Punjabi even though he had never been taught them.

Example of reincarnation

Crowds are flocking to Indian temples to see a Muslim baby who is claimed to be a reincarnation of the Hindu god Lord Hanuman. He is claimed to have a four inch tail and nine spots on his body like Lord Hanuman.

If reincarnation is true, then there is life after death.

SUMMARY

Some people believe in life after death for non-religious reasons such as:

- near-death experiences when people see things during heart attacks, operations, etc.
- evidence of the spirit world, ghosts, mediums, etc.
- evidence of reincarnation, such as people remembering previous lives.

Questions

b Do you think that some people see ghosts?
   Give two reasons for your point of view. **4**
c Explain why some people believe that the paranormal proves there is life after death. **8**
d 'The paranormal proves that there is life after death.'
   i Do you agree? Give reasons for your opinion. **3**
   ii Give reasons why some people may disagree with you. **3**

Exam Tip

d Use the answering evaluation questions advice from page 9. The arguments for can be found in this topic. The arguments against could be the quotes in the margin from Sue Blackmore, Chris Freeman, Keith Augustine and Paul Edwards. You could also use some of the arguments from Topic 2.4, page 45.

Topic 2.4 Why some people do not believe in life after death

Some people do not believe in God and believe this life is all there is. They do not believe in life after death because:

- If there is no God, there is no spirit world for life after death to happen.
- The different religions contradict each other about life after death. Christianity, Islam and Judaism say it will be resurrection or immortality of the soul; Hinduism, Sikhism and Buddhism say it will be reincarnation. If life after death were true, they would all say the same thing.
- Much of the evidence is based on holy books, but they contradict each other. There is no way of deciding which holy books are true and which false.
- The evidence of the paranormal has all been challenged by scientists (see the boxes on pages 42–43).
- Most beliefs about life after death think that the mind or soul can survive without the body. Science shows that the mind cannot live without the brain, so when the body dies, the mind must also die.
- There is no place where life after death could take place. Space journeys have shown heaven is not above the sky.
- People who have been brought up by atheists will not believe in life after death.

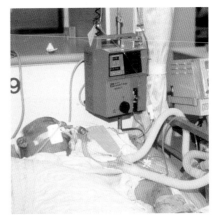

Does a person whose brain-stem is dead still have a mind or soul?

SUMMARY

Some people do not believe in life after death because:
- they do not believe in God
- there is no scientific evidence
- they do not see where life after death could take place.

Exam Tip

c 'Explain' means give reasons. To answer this question you should use four reasons from this topic, and make each of them into a short paragraph. For tips on Quality of Written Communication, look at page 3.

Questions

b Do you believe there can be a life after death? Give two reasons for your point of view. **4**
c Explain why some people do not believe in life after death. **8**
d 'When you're dead, you're dead and that's the end of you.'
　i Do you agree? Give reasons for your opinion. **3**
　ii Give reasons why some people may disagree with you. **3**

Topic 2.5 The nature of abortion

Statistics

Number of abortions carried out in England and Wales

1971	94,570
1995	154,315
1999	173,701
2001	176,364
2006	193,700

(89 per cent carried out at under 13 weeks' gestation)

Source: ONS

Pro-choice is the name given to those who support a woman's right to abortion. They do not want women to risk their lives by having operations carried out by non-doctors in bad conditions.

The law says that **abortion** is only allowed if two doctors agree:

- the mother's life is at risk
- the mother's physical or mental health is at risk
- the child is very likely to be born severely handicapped
- another child would have a serious effect on other children in the family.

Abortions cannot be carried out after 24 weeks of pregnancy, unless the mother's life is at risk or the foetus has severe handicaps.

Why abortion is a controversial issue

Abortion is a controversial issue because:

- Many people believe that life begins at the moment of conception. This means abortion is taking a human life.
- Many people believe that life begins when the foetus is able to live outside the mother. This means abortion is not taking life.

- Many non-religious people believe that a woman should have the right to do what she wants with her own body. They would argue that an unwanted foetus is no different from an unwanted tumour.
- Many religious people believe that the unborn child's right to life is greater than the mother's rights.
- Some people argue the time limit should be reduced to 18 or 20 weeks because of medical advances.
- There are also arguments about whether medical staff should have to carry out abortions.

Pro-life is the name given to those who support the foetus' right to life and want abortion banned because it denies the foetus' right to life.

If carrying out a particular procedure or giving advice about it conflicts with your religious or moral beliefs, and this conflict might affect the treatment or advice you provide, you must explain this to the patient and tell them they have the right to see another doctor ….

You must not express to your patients your personal beliefs, including political, religious or moral beliefs, in ways … that are likely to cause them distress.

Advice to doctors from *Personal Beliefs and Medical Practice* published by the General Medical Council 2008

Questions

b Do you agree with abortion? Give two reasons for your point of view. **4**

c Explain why abortion is a controversial issue. **8**

d 'Abortion is always wrong.'
   i   Do you agree? Give reasons for your opinion. **3**
   ii Give reasons why some people may disagree with you. **3**

Exam Tip

b You should already have thought about this, and you just have to give two reasons for your opinion. For example, if you agree with abortion you could use the reason of the woman's rights over her body and the foetus not being a human life until it can survive outside the womb. If you do not agree with abortion you should use two reasons against abortion from one religion.

SUMMARY

Abortion is allowed in the United Kingdom if two doctors agree that there is medical reason for it.

Abortion is a controversial issue because:

- people disagree about when life begins
- people disagree about whether abortion is murder
- people disagree about whether a woman has the right to choose.

Topic 2.6 Christian attitudes to abortion

KEY WORD

Sanctity of life – the belief that life is holy and belongs to God.

Human life must be respected and protected absolutely from the moment of conception. From the first moment of his existence, a human being must be recognised as having the rights of a person – among which is the ... right of every innocent being to life ... Abortion and infanticide are abominable crimes.

Catechism of the Catholic Church 2270–71, 2273

Before I formed you in the womb I knew you, before you were born. I set you apart; I appointed you as a prophet to the nations.

Jeremiah 1:5

Christians have two differing attitudes to abortion:

1 The Catholic Church and **Evangelical Protestant** Churches teach that all abortion is wrong whatever the circumstances because:

- Life belongs to God, so only God has the right to end a pregnancy.
- Life begins at conception so abortion is taking life and this is banned in the Ten Commandments.
- A foetus is a human being and abortion destroys its right to life.
- They believe that adoption is better than abortion as it keeps life and brings joy to a new family.
- They believe that abortion is only when the death of the foetus is intended. This means medical treatments for the mother which affect the life of the foetus are not abortion.
- They believe that counselling, help and adoption are the treatment for pregnancy as a result of rape. This means that good can come out of evil in a new life.

Out of nearly 50 million abortions carried out in the world today, 20 million are unsafe. Ninety per cent of all unsafe abortions take place in developing countries where abortion is restricted by law.

Some 70,000 women die each year as a result of unsafe abortions.

World Health Organisation statistics 2000

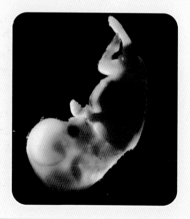

2 Other Christians (mainly **Liberal Protestants**) disagree with abortion, but think that in certain circumstances (e.g. rape, the mother's life at risk, the baby will be severely handicapped) it is necessary to choose the lesser of two evils and so abortion must be allowed. They believe abortion can be allowed in certain circumstances because:

- They do not believe that life begins at conception.
- They believe Jesus' command to love your neighbour is the most important command and abortion can be the most loving thing.
- They believe it is the duty of Christians to remove suffering.
- The **sanctity of life** can be broken in such things as a **just war**, so why not in a just abortion?
- They believe that as doctors have developed tests for certain medical conditions in unborn babies, parents should be allowed abortions if such tests show their baby would be born with serious medical problems.
- Christianity is concerned with justice. If abortions were banned, there would be one law for the rich and another for the poor.

Some Evangelical Protestants are beginning to change their attitude because they believe Jesus would have been more concerned about helping the women who want abortions than banning abortions.

Methodists would strongly prefer that through advances in medical science and social welfare, all abortions should become unnecessary. But termination as early as possible in the course of pregnancy may be the lesser of evils. If abortion were made a criminal offence again, the result would be 'one law for the rich and another for the poor', with increased risks of ill-health and death as a result of botched 'back-street' abortions.

Statement by the Methodist Church of England and Wales in *What the Churches Say*

Should abortion be legalised in areas like this where thousands of women die as a result of illegal abortions?

Questions

b Do you think abortion is murder? Give two reasons for your point of view. **4**

c Explain why some Christians allow abortion, but some do not. **8**

d 'No Christian should ever have an abortion.'
  i Do you agree? Give reasons for your opinion. **3**
  ii Give reasons why some people may disagree with you. **3**

Exam Tip

c 'Explain why' means give four brief, or two developed, reasons why some Christians do not allow abortion (Catholics and Evangelical Protestants); and four brief, or two developed, reasons why some Christians allow abortion in certain circumstances (Liberal Protestants). For tips on Quality of Written Communication, look at page 3.

SUMMARY

Christians have different attitudes to abortion:

- Some Christians believe that abortion is always wrong because it is murder and against God's will.
- Some Christians believe that abortion is wrong but must be allowed in some circumstances as the lesser of two evils.

Topic 2.7.1 Islam and abortion

> Kill not your children on a plea of want. We provide sustenance for you and for them; come not nigh to shameful deeds.
>
> **Surah 6:151**

> The jurists state that it is permissible to take medicine for abortion as long as the embryo is still unformed in human shape. The period of the unformed shape is given as 120 days. The jurists think that during this state, the embryo is not yet a human being.
>
> **Fatwa (Islamic legal decision) given by Shayqh Abdullah al'Qalqili**

SUMMARY
- Some Muslims think abortion should never be allowed.
- Some Muslims think abortion can only be allowed if the mother's life is in danger.
- Some Muslims think abortion is allowed until 120 days because this is when the foetus receives its soul.

There are different attitudes to abortion among Muslims.

1   Many Muslims allow abortions up to 120 days of pregnancy for reasons such as the health of the mother or problems with the baby's health.

They believe this because:

- Some **hadith** say a foetus does not become life until 120 days of pregnancy.
- The Shari'ah says that the mother's life must always take priority.
- Up to 120 days, the effects of the future baby on the family can be taken into account.

2   Some Muslims believe that abortion should never be allowed. They believe this because:

- They believe life begins at the moment of conception.
- The Qur'an says murder is wrong and they think abortion is murder.
- They believe that the Qur'an bans abortion.

3   Some Muslims believe that abortion can be allowed only if the mother's life is at risk. They believe this because the death of the unborn child is a lesser evil than the death of the mother. The Shari'ah says that the mother's life must always take priority.

Questions
b   Do you agree with abortion?
Give two reasons for your point of view.   **4**

c   Choose one religion other than Christianity and explain why some of the followers of that religion allow abortion and some do not.   **8**

d   'No religious person should ever have an abortion.'
  i   Do you agree? Give reasons for your opinion.   **3**
  ii   Give reasons why some people may disagree with you.   **3**

Exam Tip
d   Use the answering evaluation questions advice from page 9. The arguments for could be the Muslim reasons for abortion always being wrong plus the Christian reasons for abortion always being wrong in Topic 2.6. The arguments against could be the Muslim arguments for abortion being allowed in certain circumstances and the Christian arguments for abortion being allowed in certain circumstances in Topic 2.6.

Topic 2.7.2 Judaism and abortion

1 Some Jews believe that abortion can never be allowed because:
- They believe that life begins at conception and so abortion is murder.
- They believe in the sanctity of life and so only God has the right to take life.

> *You shall not murder.*
>
> Exodus 20:13

2 Many Jews believe that abortion is wrong, but if the mother's life is at risk, then it is permissible. They have this attitude because:
- They believe in the sanctity of life and so think abortion is wrong.
- The Torah permits killing in self-defence, and abortion is self-defence if the mother's life is at risk.

The scrolls of the Torah in the Ark. What can we learn from this picture about what most Jews believe about the Torah?

3 Some Jews believe in the UK law on abortion because:
- Life does not begin until the foetus can survive on its own.
- The Torah says that Jews must prevent avoidable suffering.
- They believe the self-defence argument for abortion.

> *See now that I myself am He! There is no god besides me. I put to death and I bring to life ...*
>
> Deuteronomy 32:39

Questions

b Do you agree with abortion? Give two reasons for your point of view. **4**

c Choose one religion other than Christianity and explain why some of the followers of that religion allow abortion and some do not. **8**

d 'No religious person should ever have an abortion.'
  i Do you agree? Give reasons for your opinion. **3**
  ii Give reasons why some people may disagree with you. **3**

Exam Tip

d Use the answering evaluation questions advice from page 9. The arguments for could be the Jewish reasons for abortion always being wrong plus the Christian reasons for abortion always being wrong in Topic 2.6. The arguments against could be the Jewish arguments for abortion being allowed in certain circumstances and the Christian arguments for abortion being allowed in certain circumstances in Topic 2.6.

SUMMARY

- Some Jews believe abortion is always wrong because life is in God's hands.
- Some Jews believe abortion can be allowed in certain circumstances because preventing suffering is taught in the Torah.

Topic 2.7.3 Hinduism and abortion

> *Do not have an abortion and do not keep the company of women who have. Do not keep the company of a woman who encourages or assists in abortion.*
>
> **Shikshapatri of Lord Swaminarayan**

> *Unborn, eternal, everlasting, he (the soul), primeval: he is not slain when the body is slain. If a man knows him as indestructible, eternal, unborn, never to pass away, how and whom can he cause to be slain or slay.*
>
> **Bhagavad Gita 2:20–21**

There are different attitudes to abortion in Hinduism.

1   Some Hindus believe that abortion is always wrong because:
  • Some **Gurus** have said that all abortion is wrong.
  • They believe that taking life gives bad karma.

2   Some Hindus believe that abortion is only allowed if the mother's life is at risk because:
  • Hindu teachings on **ahimsa** say that violence can be used as a final choice.
  • If the foetus threatens the sanctity of the mother's life abortion is acceptable.

3   Some British Hindus allow abortion according to the UK law because:
  • The teachings of the Bhagavad Gita mean that abortion will not affect karma.
  • They believe that life does not begin until the foetus can survive outside the womb.

Abortion is available on demand in India where about five million abortions a year are carried out (83 per cent of India's population is Hindu).

Questions

b   Do you agree with abortion? Give two reasons for your point of view.   **4**

c   Choose one religion other than Christianity and explain why some of the followers of that religion allow abortion and some do not.   **8**

d   'No religious person should ever have an abortion.'
  i   Do you agree? Give reasons for your opinion.   **3**
  ii Give reasons why some people may disagree with you.   **3**

Exam Tip

d   Use the answering evaluation questions advice from page 9. The arguments for could be the Hindu reasons for abortion always being wrong plus the Christian reasons for abortion always being wrong in Topic 2.6. The arguments against could be the Hindu arguments for abortion being allowed in certain circumstances and the Christian arguments for abortion being allowed in certain circumstances in Topic 2.6.

SUMMARY

• Some Hindus think abortion should never be allowed.
• Some Hindus think abortion can only be allowed if the mother's life is in danger.
• Some Hindus think abortion is allowed in any circumstances.

Topic 2.7.4 Sikhism and abortion

There are different attitudes to abortion in Sikhism.

1   Some Sikhs believe that abortion can only be used if the mother's life is in danger or she has been raped because:
   - They believe life is sacred and begins at conception, so abortion is wrong.
   - They believe only God has the right to take life.
   - They believe in the lesser of two evils. They believe the death of the foetus is less evil than the death of the mother.

2   Some British Sikhs allow abortion according to UK law. They believe this because:
   - Each individual is part of God's essence so they believe the mother has rights over the foetus.
   - They believe sanctity of life involves the lives of the mother and other family members as well as the life of the foetus. It also involves the removal of suffering.

> *A child is born when it pleases God.*
>
> **Guru Granth Sahib 921**

> *Cursed is he who kills a daughter.*
>
> **Guru Granth Sahib 1413**

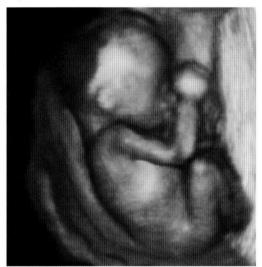

Killing girl children was condemned by the Ten Gurus. Many modern Sikhs use this teaching to condemn those who have an abortion when scans show the foetus is female.

Questions

b   Do you agree with abortion? Give two reasons for your point of view.   **4**

c   Choose one religion other than Christianity and explain why some of the followers of that religion allow abortion and some do not.   **8**

d   'No religious person should ever have an abortion.'
   i   Do you agree? Give reasons for your opinion.   **3**
   ii Give reasons why some people may disagree with you.   **3**

Exam Tip

d   Use the answering evaluation questions advice from page 9. The arguments for could be the Sikh reasons for abortion always being wrong plus the Christian reasons for abortion always being wrong in Topic 2.6. The arguments against could be the Sikh arguments for abortion being allowed in certain circumstances and the Christian arguments for abortion being allowed in certain circumstances in Topic 2.6.

SUMMARY

- Many Sikhs believe abortion is wrong except for when the mother's life is at risk or she has been raped.
- Some Sikhs believe in the UK law on abortion because they believe sanctity of life involves removing suffering.

Topic 2.8 The nature of euthanasia

KEY WORDS

Assisted suicide – providing a seriously ill person with the means to commit suicide.

Euthanasia – the painless killing of someone dying from a painful disease.

Non-voluntary euthanasia – ending someone's life painlessly when they are unable to ask, but you have good reason for thinking they would want you to do so.

Quality of life – the idea that life must have some benefits for it to be worth living.

Voluntary euthanasia – ending life painlessly when someone in great pain asks for death.

Euthanasia is normally thought of as providing a gentle and easy death to someone suffering from a painful, deadly disease who has little **quality of life**. This can be done by: **assisted suicide**, **voluntary euthanasia**, **non-voluntary euthanasia**.

British law says that all these methods of euthanasia are murder. However, the law now agrees that stopping artificial feeding or not giving treatment (often called passive euthanasia) are not euthanasia and so are lawful.

Why euthanasia is a controversial issue

1 Many people want euthanasia to remain illegal because:

- There is always likely to be doubt as to whether it is what the person really wants.
- There is also the problem as to whether the disease will end the life. A cure might be found for the disease.
- It is the job of doctors to save lives, not end them. Would patients trust doctors who kill their patients?
- People might change their mind, but then it would be too late.
- Who would check that they were only killing people who really wanted and needed euthanasia?

2 Many people want euthanasia to be made legal because:

- Discoveries in medicine mean that people who would have died are being kept alive, often in agony. They should have the right to die.

- Doctors have the right to switch off life-support machines if they think the patient has no chance of recovering, and allow people who have been in a coma for years to die. So euthanasia is already legal.
- People have a right to commit suicide, so why not give them the right to ask doctors to assist their suicide if they are too weak to do it alone?
- Just as doctors can now switch off life-support machines, so judges have said that doctors can stop treatment.

Nancy Crick was assisted to commit suicide by right-to-die campaigners because she had terminal cancer. After her death it was discovered that she was in remission. Her relatives and the campaigners still believe it was right. Her son said, 'It makes little difference whether she had cancer or not. Our main concern is that our mother is at peace.'

Questions

b Do you agree with euthanasia? Give two reasons for your point of view. **4**

c Explain why euthanasia is a controversial issue. **8**

d 'The law on euthanasia should be changed.'
  i Do you agree? Give reasons for your opinion. **3**
  ii Give reasons why some people may disagree with you. **3**

Exam Tip

b You should already have thought about this, and you just have to give two reasons for your opinion. For example, if you don't agree with euthanasia, you could use the reasons of unscrupulous relatives and doctors having a duty to save lives, not kill.

SUMMARY

There are various types of euthanasia that are all aimed at giving an easy death to those suffering intolerably.

British law says that euthanasia is a crime, but withholding treatment to dying patients is not.

Topic 2.9 Christian attitudes to euthanasia

The use of painkillers to alleviate the suffering of the dying, even at the risk of shortening their days, can be morally in conformity with human dignity if death is not willed either as an end or a means, but only foreseen and tolerated as inevitable.

Catechism of the Catholic Church 2279

If we live, we live to the Lord; and if we die, we die to the Lord. So, whether we live or die, we belong to the Lord.

Romans 14:8

Discontinuing medical procedures that are burdensome, dangerous, extraordinary, or disproportionate to the expected outcome can be legitimate; it is the refusal of 'over-zealous' treatment.

Catechism of the Catholic Church 2278

Although all Christians believe that euthanasia is wrong, there are slightly different attitudes:

1 Catholics and many Liberal Protestants believe that assisted suicide, voluntary euthanasia and non-voluntary euthanasia are all wrong. However, they believe that the switching off of life-support machines, not giving treatment that could cause distress and giving dying people painkillers are not euthanasia. They have this attitude because:

- They believe in the sanctity of life. Life is created by God and so it is up to God, not humans, when people die.
- They regard euthanasia as murder, which is forbidden in the Ten Commandments.
- If doctors say someone is brain-dead, then they have already died, so switching off the machine is accepting what God has already decided.
- If you give painkillers to a dying person in great pain, and they kill the person, this is not murder because your intention was to remove their pain, not to kill them (doctrine of double effect).
- Not giving extraordinary treatment is permitted by the **Catechism** – see Catechism 2278 quote on the left.

2 Some Christians believe any form of euthanasia is wrong, including the switching off of life-support machines, the refusal of treatment or the giving of large doses of painkillers. They have this attitude because:

- They take the Bible teachings literally and the Bible bans suicide.
- Euthanasia includes the switching off of life-support machines, the refusal of treatment and giving large doses of painkillers because life is being ended by humans not God.
- All forms of euthanasia are murder, which is banned by the Ten Commandments.

- They believe that life is sacred and should only be taken by God. The Bible says that life and death decisions belong to God alone.

3   A few Christians accept euthanasia in certain circumstances because:

- Medical advances mean it is hard to know what God's wishes about someone's death are.
- The teaching of Jesus on loving your neighbour can be used to justify assisting suicide.
- It is a basic human right to be in control of your own body.

The common experience of Christians throughout the ages has been that the grace of God sustains heart and mind to the end. To many, the end of life is clouded by pain and impaired judgement, and whilst we believe that it is right to use all and any medical treatment to control pain, experience denies the rightness of legalising the termination of life by a doctor, authorised by a statement signed by the patient whilst in health. Such euthanasia threatens to debase the function of doctors and impairs the confidence of their patients.

Statement by the Salvation Army in *What the Churches Say on Moral Issues*

Many Christians help in the running of hospices to ease the suffering and death of the terminally ill without euthanasia.

Questions

b   Do you think switching off a life-support machine is euthanasia? Give two reasons for your point of view.   **4**

c   Explain two different Christian attitudes to euthanasia.   **8**

d   'Life belongs to God and should only be taken by God.'
  i   Do you agree? Give reasons for your opinion.   **3**
  ii   Give reasons why some people may disagree with you.   **3**

Exam Tip

d   Use the answering evaluation questions advice from page 9. The arguments for could come from the Christian arguments against euthanasia. The arguments against could be from Topic 2.8 reasons for allowing euthanasia.

SUMMARY

All Christians are against euthanasia because they believe life is sacred and belongs to God.

However, there are some different attitudes among Christians about switching off life-support machines, withdrawing treatment, and so on, because some think these are not euthanasia.

Topic 2.10.1 Islam and euthanasia

The Prophet said, 'In the time before you, a man was wounded. His wounds troubled him so much that he took a knife and cut his wrist to bleed himself to death.' Thereupon Allah said, 'My slave hurried in the matter of his life, therefore he is deprived of the Garden.'

Hadith reported in al'Burkhari

Nor can a soul die except by God's leave, the term being fixed as by writing.

Surah 3:145

All Muslims are against euthanasia, but there are two slightly different attitudes.

1   Most Muslims are against all forms of euthanasia because:

- The Qur'an bans suicide and so assisted suicide is wrong.
- Most Muslims believe that voluntary euthanasia is just the same as assisted suicide.
- Euthanasia is making yourself equal with God as only God has the right to take life. So euthanasia could be the greatest sin of **shirk**.
- Euthanasia is murder, which is banned by the Qur'an.
- Muslims believe that life is a test from God. So if people use euthanasia, they are cheating in the test by trying to speed it up.

2   Some Muslims agree that euthanasia is wrong, but think switching off life-support machines is not euthanasia because:

- Some Muslim lawyers have agreed to life-support machines being switched off when there are no signs of life.
- If someone is brain-dead, God has already taken their life.

SUMMARY

All Muslims are against euthanasia because they believe life is sacred and belongs to God. However, there are some different attitudes among Muslims about the switching off of life-support machines, withdrawing treatment, and so on, because some think these are not euthanasia.

Questions

b   Do you think suicide is always wrong? Give two reasons for your point of view.   **4**

c   Choose one religion other than Christianity and explain why most of the followers of that religion are against euthanasia.   **8**

d   'Euthanasia is always wrong.'
   i   Do you agree? Give reasons for your opinion.   **3**
   ii   Give reasons why some people may disagree with you.   **3**

Exam Tip

c   'Explain why' means you should use four reasons why Muslims are against euthanasia, and make each of them into a short paragraph. For tips on Quality of Written Communication, look at page 3.

Topic 2.10.2 Judaism and euthanasia

Judaism is against euthanasia, but there are two slightly different attitudes among Jewish people.

1 Most Jews do not allow euthanasia because:

- The Torah bans suicide and so assisted suicide is wrong.
- Many Jewish people believe that voluntary euthanasia is just the same as assisted suicide.
- Murder is banned by the **Ten Commandments** and euthanasia is a form of murder.
- The Tenakh say that death and life are in the hands of God.

2 Some Jews believe euthanasia is wrong. However, they believe switching off life-support machines or not 'striving to keep alive' is not wrong. They believe this because:

- Some rabbis have said switching off life-support for the brain-dead is not euthanasia.
- If someone is brain-dead, God has already taken their life.
- Striving to keep someone alive is preventing God from taking their soul and so is against God's wishes.

> Naked I came from my mother's womb, and naked I shall depart. The Lord gave and the Lord has taken away; may the name of the Lord be praised.
>
> **Job 1:21**

> If there is anything which causes a hindrance to the departure of the soul ... then it is permissible to remove it.
>
> **Rabbi Moses Isserles**

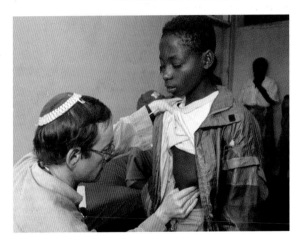

What do you think the attitude of this Jewish doctor might be to euthanasia and switching off life-support machines?

Questions

b Do you think suicide is always wrong? Give two reasons for your point of view. **4**

c Choose one religion other than Christianity and explain why most of the followers of that religion are against euthanasia. **8**

d 'Euthanasia is always wrong.'
  i Do you agree? Give reasons for your opinion. **3**
  ii Give reasons why some people may disagree with you. **3**

Exam Tip

c 'Explain why' means you should use four reasons why Jewish people are against euthanasia, and make each of them into a short paragraph. For tips on Quality of Written Communication, look at page 3.

SUMMARY

Judaism is against euthanasia because it teaches that life is sacred and belongs to God. However, there are some different attitudes among Jewish people about switching off life-support machines, withdrawing treatment, and so on, because some think these are not euthanasia.

Topic 2.10.3 Hinduism and euthanasia

Radha being persuaded to meet Lord Krishna. Does the teaching of Lord Krishna in the Bhagavad Gita, that killing the body cannot harm the soul, justify euthanasia?

> *Non-violence is the highest ethical code of behaviour. It includes non-killing, non-injury and non-harming. Do not kill any living creature ... Do not kill a human being ... Do not commit suicide.*
>
> **Shikshapatri of Lord Swaminarayan**

> *Unborn, eternal, everlasting he (the soul) primeval: he is not slain when the body is slain.*
>
> **Bhagavad Gita 2:20**

There are different attitudes to euthanasia in Hinduism.

1   Some Hindus are against all forms of euthanasia because:

- The teaching on ahimsa means that euthanasia is unacceptable because it must involve inflicting violence.
- Euthanasia would damage a soul and bring bad karma, stopping the soul from gaining moksha.
- According to the law of karma, God alone must give and take life at the right time.
- The **Laws of Manu** say that murder is wrong.

2   Some Hindus believe that euthanasia can be allowed in certain circumstances. Not only switching off life-support machines and not striving to keep someone alive are permitted, but also when there is no quality of life. They have this attitude because:

- If someone is brain-dead, God has already taken their life and so switching off the machine would not be euthanasia.
- The Bhagavad Gita teaches that the soul cannot be harmed.
- Refusing euthanasia when there is no quality of life is a form of violence and so is against ahimsa.
- Striving to keep alive is preventing the soul from moving on to moksha or its next life.

SUMMARY

- Some Hindus agree with euthanasia if the dying person wants to die easily because it releases the soul.
- Other Hindus only allow life-support machines to be switched off and no other form of euthanasia because life is sacred.

Questions

b   Do you think suicide is always wrong? Give two reasons for your point of view.   **4**

c   Choose one religion other than Christianity and explain why most of the followers of that religion are against euthanasia.   **8**

d   'Euthanasia is always wrong.'

　i   Do you agree? Give reasons for your opinion.   **3**

　ii   Give reasons why some people may disagree with you.   **3**

Exam Tip

c   'Explain why' means you should use four reasons why some Hindus are against euthanasia, and make each of them into a short paragraph. For tips on Quality of Written Communication, look at page 3.

Topic 2.10.4 Sikhism and euthanasia

Sikhism is against euthanasia, but there are two slightly different attitudes among Sikh people.

1 Most Sikhs are against all forms of euthanasia because:

   - Sikh teaching on violence to humans means that euthanasia would bring bad **karma** and prevent mukti.
   - According to the **law of karma**, God alone must give and take life at the right time.
   - The **Rahit Maryada** says that murder is wrong.
   - Euthanasia would be damaging a soul, which is condemned in the Guru Granth Sahib.
   - To practise euthanasia is making oneself equal to God, the worst form of manmukh. This would create a massive amount of bad karma.

2 Many Sikhs are against euthanasia but allow the switching off of life-support machines and not striving to keep alive because:

   - If someone is brain-dead their life has already ended, so it is not being taken.
   - Striving to keep alive is preventing the soul from moving on, so it is stopping the law of karma.
   - Release of the soul is the aim of Sikh life, so people should not be kept alive artificially.

> *God sends us and we take birth. God calls us back and we die.*
>
> Guru Granth Sahib 1239

> *The dawn of a new day is the herald of a sunset. Earth is not your permanent home.*
>
> Guru Granth Sahib 793

SUMMARY

- Most Sikhs are against euthanasia because they believe life and death should be in the hands of God, and that killing brings bad karma and so will prevent mukti.
- Some Sikhs accept not striving to keep someone alive and switching off life-support machines because not to do so would prevent the release of the soul.

Questions

b Do you think suicide is always wrong? Give two reasons for your point of view. **4**

c Choose one religion other than Christianity and explain why most of the followers of that religion are against euthanasia. **8**

d 'Euthanasia is always wrong.'
   i Do you agree? Give reasons for your opinion. **3**
   ii Give reasons why some people may disagree with you. **3**

Exam Tip

c 'Explain why' means you should use four reasons why most Sikhs are against euthanasia, and make each of them into a short paragraph. For tips on Quality of Written Communication, look at page 3.

Topic 2.11 The media and matters of life and death

Forms of communication.

The media are all forms of communication, including newspapers, television, radio, films and the internet. Note that the word is plural.

Religion makes many statements in the media about such matters of life and death as abortion, euthanasia, transplants, genetic engineering, cloning and fertility treatments.

You need to know arguments for and against the media being free to criticise these statements.

1. Arguments that the media should not be free to criticise what religions say about matters of life and death

- Some people believe that criticising what religions say on matters of life and death is a way of stirring up religious hatred. This is banned by the Racial and Religious Hatred Act, 2007. For example, when the Catholic Church told Catholics to withdraw their support from Amnesty International because Amnesty had decided abortion should be a human right for women who had been raped, the media reports chose examples that were bound to show the Catholic position in a bad light.
- Many religious believers believe the freedom of the media should be limited because of the offence criticism of religious attitudes can bring.
  For example, when a Danish newspaper published cartoons of the Prophet Muhammad, there were riots in some countries. (See the photo on page 63.)

In 2006 a Danish newspaper printed cartoons of the Prophet Muhammad, which caused worldwide protest by Muslims who believe the prophet should not be pictured. This picture shows Pakistanis at a protest rally. Do you think that there should be total freedom of speech, or that the media should not cause offence?

- Some religious believers believe that criticising what religious leaders say about matters of life and death is close to the crime of blasphemy. If the media criticise the Pope's teachings on a topic like abortion, they are condemning the Catholic Church.
  The last trial on the blasphemy law was in 1977, when the trial judge said using words that were insulting, abusive or offensive to Christianity was blasphemous libel.
- Some religious people feel that religious statements are based on what God says and so are beyond human criticism.

It is deeply misguided to propose a law by which it would be legal for the terminally ill to be killed or assisted in suicide by those caring for them, even if there are safeguards to ensure it is only the terminally ill who would qualify. To take this step would fundamentally undermine the basis of law and medicine and undermine the duty of the state to care for vulnerable people ... As a result many who are ill or dying would feel a burden to others. The right to die would become the duty to die.

Part of a joint submission by all the Church of England and Catholic bishops to the House of Lords Select Committee on the Assisted Dying for the Terminally Ill Bill. Should the media have a right to criticise such statements?

2. Arguments that the media should be free to criticise what religions say about matters of life and death

- Freedom of expression is a basic human right which is needed for democracy to work. Before people vote they need to know what is going on in the world and in their own country. For this they need a free media, and if the media have freedom of expression, then they must be free to criticise religious attitudes to matters of life and death.

- If religious leaders use the media to make statements about matters of life and death (as they do on things like stem cell research), they must be prepared for the media to criticise those statements.

- In a **multi-faith society** such as the United Kingdom, there must be freedom of religious belief and expression. This means that the media must have the right to question and even criticise not only religious beliefs, but also what religions say about life and death issues.

- Life and death issues are so important to everyone that people want to know what is the right view. This could not be done if religions were allowed to put forward views that no one could criticise.

Mongolians voting in the fifth general election since democracy was established in the 1990s. Do voters need a free press to be able to cast their votes properly?

- Sir Karl Popper, a great twentieth-century philosopher, claimed that the societies with the greatest freedoms for their citizens are the most advanced. This is because progress is made by allowing criticism of all ideas, policies and so on, discovering what is false in them and then putting forward a more correct version. This can only happen if government policies and religious attitudes can be criticised by a free media.

Sir Karl Popper.

Questions

b Do you think the media should be free to criticise religion? Give two reasons for your point of view. **4**

c Explain why people argue about the way the media treat religion. **8**

d 'The media should not criticise religious attitudes to abortion.'
   i   Do you agree? Give reasons for your opinion. **3**
   ii Give reasons why some people may disagree with you. **3**

Exam Tip

d Use the answering evaluation questions advice from page 9. The arguments for could be three of the reasons from point 1 of this topic. Arguments against could be three of the reasons from point 2 of this topic.

SUMMARY

Some people think that what religions say about matters of life and death should not be criticised by the media because:

- They might stir up religious hatred.
- They might be offensive to religious believers.

Other people think the media should be free to criticise religious attitudes because:

- A free media is a key part of democracy.
- If religions want to be free to say what they want, then the media must also be free to criticise religion.

How to answer exam questions

Question A What is non-voluntary euthanasia?   2 marks

Ending someone's life painlessly when they are unable to ask, but you have good reason for thinking they would want you to do so.

Question B Do you agree with abortion?
Give two reasons for your point of view.   4 marks

Yes I do agree with abortion because I don't think a foetus is a human life until it is capable of living outside the mother. Therefore abortions before 24 weeks are not taking life. I also believe that a woman should have the right to do what she wants with her own body. The problems caused to a woman by having an unwanted baby justify her having an abortion.

Question C Choose one religion other than Christianity and explain why most of its followers are against euthanasia.   8 marks

Muslims are mainly against euthanasia because in the Qur'an it teaches that humans are one of Allah's greatest creations and so to take away Allah's creation is a sin. Muslims regard the Qur'an as the word of Allah and so they must obey what the Qur'an says.

Muslims also believe that life is a test from Allah, so if someone is terminally ill they should not be relieved of their pain as it is a test of their faith in Allah. If they stay true to Allah they will be rewarded for that with an afterlife in eternal paradise. Therefore to commit euthanasia is not necessary as people will be relieved of their suffering in Allah's own way.

Another reason is that most Muslims regard any type of euthanasia as a form of murder. As murder is totally forbidden in the Qur'an, no Muslims should commit or allow euthanasia.

Muslims also believe in the sanctity of life, that life is precious and a gift from Allah. This means that no one has the authority to take away life but Allah, as he is the one who created it, therefore euthanasia is wrong.

Question D 'Your soul will never die.'

i Do you agree? Give reasons for your opinion.   3 marks

ii Give reasons why some people may disagree with you.   3 marks

i I disagree. I don't see how the soul can live on after the death of the brain. What is your soul if it is not the brain? The evidence of science is that the human mind developed as the brain grew more complex, and so the mind cannot exist without the brain (for example, people who are brain-dead on a life-support machine). Also, where would souls live after the death of the body? Space exploration has shown there is no heaven above the sky and physics has shown there is no non-material world on earth. Finally there is no evidence for souls living after death. All the evidence for the paranormal is capable of being disproven.
ii Christians might disagree with me because they believe there is life after death because Jesus rose from the dead. Also it is part of the creeds to believe in the life everlasting, which means the soul cannot die. They might quote as evidence that Jesus said to one of the robbers crucified with him, 'This day you will be with me in paradise.' They take this to mean that the robber's soul would not die at the crucifixion but live on in heaven.

QUESTION A
A high mark answer because it is a correct definition of the key word.

QUESTION B
A high mark answer because an opinion is backed up by two developed reasons.

QUESTION C
A high mark answer because four reasons for Muslims being against euthanasia are developed. A formal style of English is used and there is good use of specialist vocabulary – Qur'an, Allah, creation, test of faith, eternal paradise, sanctity of life.

QUESTION D
A high mark answer because it states the candidate's own opinion and backs it up with three clear reasons for thinking that the soul will die. It then gives three reasons for people disagreeing and believing that the soul will never die.

Section 3 **Marriage and the family**

Introduction

This section of the examination specification requires you to look at issues surrounding sex and marriage, divorce, family life, homosexuality and contraception.

Sex and marriage
You will need to understand the effects of, and give reasons for your own opinion about:
- changing attitudes to marriage, divorce, family life and homosexuality
- attitudes to sex outside marriage in Christianity
- attitudes to sex outside marriage in one religion other than Christianity.

Divorce
You will need to understand the effects of, and give reasons for your own opinion about:
- different Christian attitudes to divorce and the reasons for them
- different attitudes to divorce in one religion other than Christianity, and the reasons for them.

Family life
You will need to understand the effects of, and give reasons for your own opinion about:
- Christian teachings on family life and its importance
- the teachings of one religion other than Christianity on family life and its importance.

Homosexuality
You will need to understand the effects of, and give reasons for your own opinion about:
- Christian attitudes to homosexuality and the reasons for them
- attitudes to homosexuality in one religion other than Christianity, and the reasons for them.

Contraception
You will need to understand the effects of, and give reasons for your own opinion about:
- different Christian attitudes to contraception and the reasons for them
- different attitudes to contraception in one religion other than Christianity, and the reasons for them.

Topic 3.1 Changing attitudes to marriage and family life

KEY WORDS

Civil partnership – a legal ceremony giving a homosexual couple the same legal rights as a husband and wife.

Cohabitation – living together without being married.

Nuclear family – mother, father and children living as a unit.

Re-constituted family – where two sets of children (step-brothers and step-sisters) become one family when their divorced parents marry each other.

The British Social Attitudes Survey 2008 revealed these facts about what people think:

- 66% of people think there is little difference between marriage and living together

- 48% think that living with a partner shows just as much commitment as marriage

- 72% think unmarried couples are just as good parents as married ones

- 78% think that conflict between parents is more harmful to children than divorce

- 75% think that a mother and step-father can bring up children just as well as the biological parents

In the United Kingdom in the 1960s:

- people were expected to only have sex after marriage
- people married young, in church, for life
- families were husband and wife and children
- male **homosexuality** was a criminal offence.

How attitudes have changed

- Most people have sex before marriage.
- Many couples live together (**cohabit**) rather than marry.
- The average age for marrying has increased enormously.
- Most marriages do not take place in church.
- Divorce is accepted as a normal part of life.
- There is much more divorce. This means there are more single-parent families and **re-constituted families**.
- There are more extended families as more mothers are in paid employment and grandparents look after their children.
- More children are being brought up by cohabiting parents.
- Society treats homosexual sex the same way as heterosexual sex.

Do you think this **nuclear family** would be any different if the parents were cohabiting rather than being married?

- Two people of the same sex can now form a legal union by signing a registration document in a **civil partnership**. This gives them the same rights and treatment as an opposite-sex married couple.

Reasons for the changes

Cohabitation and marriage

- Effective **contraception** made it safer to have sex before marriage.
- Fewer people went to church and so were not encouraged to keep sex until after marriage.
- The media and celebrities made cohabitation look respectable and so it become more popular.
- The media showed sexual relationships outside marriage as the norm so more people thought sex outside marriage was OK.

Divorce

- New laws made divorce much cheaper and easier for ordinary people.
- Increased equality for women means that women are no longer prepared to accept unequal treatment from men. If their husbands treat them badly, they will divorce them.
- Most married women depended on the husband's wages. Now many women are financially independent and can support themselves after a divorce.
- There has been a great change in how long people are likely to be married. Most divorces occur after ten years of marriage. This was the average length of a marriage 100 years ago.

In 2005, the government and the Church agreed to the marriage of Prince Charles to Camilla Parker Bowles, even though both had been divorced.

Most cohabiting couples think that they have the same rights about financial support, property, children, and so on, as they would if they were married, but this is not the case. The law that currently applies to such couples (cohabiting couples) on separation is unclear and complicated, and it can produce unfair outcomes. This causes serious hardship not only to cohabitants themselves, but also to their children.

Statement from the Law Commission about proposals to give legal rights to cohabiting couples that were shelved in March 2008

Changing attitudes and STDs

Some people think that the changing attitudes to sex and marriage have led to a large increase in sexually transmitted diseases. Cases of sexually transmitted diseases rose by 63 per cent between 1997 and 2006.

ONS

KEY WORDS

Homosexuality – sexual attraction to the same sex.

Re-marriage – marrying again after being divorced from a previous marriage.

SUMMARY

Fifty years ago, most people only had sex in marriage, and they married in church. Now, people have sex before they marry, cohabiting is acceptable and most marriages are not in church. This could be caused by safer contraception and fewer people being influenced by religion.

Divorce and re-marriage used to be rare but are accepted today, and two in five marriages end in divorce. The changes may have been caused by cheaper divorce and women having more equality.

Family life has changed so that, although most children are still brought up by a mother and a father, the parents may not be married or they may have been married more than once. These changes are probably caused by the changing attitudes to sex, marriage and divorce.

Homosexuality used to be illegal, but now homosexuals have the same rights to sexual activity as heterosexuals including civil partnerships. These changes are probably due to discoveries showing homosexuality is natural and changes to the law.

Family life

- The popularity of cohabitation means there are more families where the parents are not married.
- The increase in divorce has led to an increase in **re-marriage** and so there are now many more re-constituted families.
- More mothers are in paid employment and use retired grandparents or close relatives to look after their children.
- The increase in divorce and the acceptance of unmarried mothers means there are more single-parent families.

Homosexuality

- Changes in the laws have made it easier for homosexuals and made people aware of **homosexuality**.
- Medical research has shown that homosexuality is 'normal', leading people to accept homosexual couples.
- Media coverage of gay celebrities has led to a greater acceptance of all gay people.
- The work of gay rights groups has led to an acceptance of equal rights for homosexuals.

Elton John and David Furnish on the day they formed their civil partnership. Do you think civil partnerships are a good idea?

Questions

b Do you think homosexuals should be allowed to marry? Give two reasons for your point of view. **4**

c Explain why attitudes to marriage and divorce have changed. **8**

d 'There's no difference between living with a partner and being married to them.'
   i Do you agree? Give reasons for your opinion. **3**
   ii Give reasons why some people may disagree with you. **3**

Exam Tip

c 'Explain' means give reasons. To answer this question you should use two reasons from cohabitation and marriage and two from divorce, and make each of them into a short paragraph. For tips on Quality of Written Communication, look at page 3.

Topic 3.2 Christian attitudes to sex outside marriage

Most Christians believe sex outside marriage is wrong because:

- God gave sex for the **procreation** of children, who should be brought up in a Christian family, so sex should only take place within marriage.
- The Bible says that sex outside marriage is sinful and Christians should follow the teachings of the Bible.
- The Catechism says that **pre-marital sex** is wrong and Catholics should follow the teachings of the Catechism.
- All Christians are against **adultery** because it breaks the wedding vows.
- Adultery is also banned by the Ten Commandments, which all Christians should follow.
- Adultery is condemned by Jesus and all Christians should follow the teachings of Jesus.

Some Christians accept that couples may live together before marriage, but only in a long-term relationship leading to marriage.

> **KEY WORDS**
>
> **Adultery** – a sexual act between a married person and someone other than their marriage partner.
>
> **Faithfulness** – staying with your marriage partner and having sex only with them.
>
> **Pre-marital sex** – sex before marriage.
>
> **Procreation** – making a new life.
>
> **Promiscuity** – having sex with a number of partners without commitment.

> *The sexual act must always take place ... within marriage ... Human love does not tolerate 'trial marriages'. It demands a total ... gift of persons to one another.*
>
> **Catechism of the Catholic Church 2390–91**

> *Cohabiting couples should be welcomed and supported by the Church, 'recognising that for many this is a step along the way to the fuller commitment of marriage'.*
>
> *Something to Celebrate*
> **A report published by the Church of England's Board of Responsibility in 1995**

SUMMARY
- All Christians believe adultery is wrong as it breaks one of the Ten Commandments.
- Most Christians believe that sex before marriage is wrong because the Church and the Bible teach this.

Exam Tip
c 'Explain' means give reasons. To answer this question you should use two reasons against pre-marital sex and two reasons against adultery, and make each of them into a short paragraph. For tips on Quality of Written Communication, look at page 3.

Questions
b Do you think Christians should be allowed to have sex before marriage? Give two reasons for your point of view. **4**
c Explain why most Christians are against sex outside marriage. **8**
d 'Christians should never have sex outside marriage.'
   i Do you agree? Give reasons for your opinion. **3**
   ii Give reasons why some people may disagree with you. **3**

Topic 3.3.1 Islam and sex outside marriage

Because Islam emphasises chastity and modesty, there is normally very little contact between young Muslim men and women ... there is no such thing as dating or pre-marital intimacy of any kind. In Islam, sexual behaviour and acts are only for those legally married.

From *What Does Islam Say?* by I. Hewitt

The woman and the man guilty of adultery and fornication, flog each of them with a hundred stripes: let not compassion move you in a matter prescribed by God.

Surah 24:2

SUMMARY

Muslims believe that sex before marriage and adultery are both wrong because the Qur'an teaches this.

Muslims believe that sex outside marriage is wrong because:

- Sex before marriage is forbidden by the Qur'an, and Muslims believe the Qur'an is the word of God.
- The Shari'ah says that sex should only take place in marriage.
- Islam teaches that sex is for the procreation of children who should be raised in a family where the mother and father are married.
- Adultery is condemned by God in the Qur'an.
- Adultery breaks the marriage contract that both husband and wife agreed to.
- Adultery is likely to harm the family, and harming the family is condemned by both the Qur'an and Shari'ah.

Young people holding hands. Why do you think some Muslim parents would forbid this?

Questions

b Do you think sex before marriage is wrong? Give two reasons for your point of view. **4**

c Choose one religion other than Christianity and explain why its followers are against sex outside marriage. **8**

d 'No religious person should ever have sex outside marriage.'

   i Do you agree? Give reasons for your opinion. **3**

   ii Give reasons why some people may disagree with you. **3**

Exam Tip

c 'Explain' means give reasons. To answer this question you should use two reasons against pre-marital sex and two reasons against adultery, and make each of them into a short paragraph. For tips on Quality of Written Communication, look at page 3.

Topic 3.3.2 Judaism and sex outside marriage

Jewish people believe that sex outside marriage is wrong because:

- Sex before marriage is forbidden by the Torah, which all Jewish people should follow.
- The Talmud says that sex should only take place in marriage so Jewish people should avoid sex outside marriage.
- Judaism teaches that sex is for the procreation of children who should be raised in a family where the mother and father are married.
- Adultery is banned by the Ten Commandments, which all Jewish people should follow.
- Adultery breaks the marriage contract that both husband and wife agreed to.
- Adultery is likely to harm the family, which should not be harmed as it is where children learn about Judaism and how to live the Jewish life.

Some **Progressive Jews** accept that couples may live together before marriage, but only in a long-term relationship leading to marriage.

The Torah lists the forbidden sexual relationships and then says, 'You shall be Holy' (Leviticus 19:2). This tells you that even in a permitted relationship, you must sanctify yourself (keep yourself holy).

Rabbi Moses ben Nachman 1194–1270

Judaism teaches that sexuality plays an important role in human relationships. However, it also recognises that the sexual urge can generate very powerful emotions, and that for this reason sexual behaviour must be carefully regulated.

From *Moral Issues in Judaism*

A Jewish school for boys. Why do you think there are no girls at this school?

Questions

b Do you think sex before marriage is wrong? Give two reasons for your point of view. **4**

c Choose one religion other than Christianity and explain why its followers are against sex outside marriage. **8**

d 'No religious person should ever have sex outside marriage.'
  i Do you agree? Give reasons for your opinion. **3**
  ii Give reasons why some people may disagree with you. **3**

Exam Tip

c 'Explain' means give reasons. To answer this question you should use two reasons against pre-marital sex and two reasons against adultery, and make each of them into a short paragraph. For tips on Quality of Written Communication, look at page 3.

SUMMARY

- All Jews believe adultery is wrong as it breaks one of the Ten Commandments.
- Most Jews believe that sex before marriage is wrong because the Torah teaches this.
- Some Jews believe that sex before marriage can be accepted with certain conditions.

Topic 3.3.3 Hinduism and sex outside marriage

Hinduism emphasises the positive value of human sexuality, and by showing ideal relationships (for example between Krishna and Radha, or between Rama and Sita) it offers an image of religious devotion and examples for people to follow.

From *Guidelines for Life* by Mel Thompson

O married men and women; be loving and faithful to one another.

Shikshapatri of Lord Swaminarayan

Hindus believe that sex outside marriage is wrong because:

- Sex is not allowed in the student stage of life so sex before marriage would prevent you from gaining moksha.
- The Hindu scriptures say that sex should only take place in marriage.
- Hinduism teaches that sex is for the procreation of children who should be raised in a family where the mother and father are married.
- Committing adultery is betraying your **dharma**, which prevents your soul from achieving moksha.
- Adultery is a betrayal of the marriage partner and betrayal brings bad karma.
- Adultery is likely to harm the family, which should not be harmed as it is where children learn to be good Hindus.

Rama and Sita are regarded as an ideal Hindu married couple who were faithful to each other.

SUMMARY

Hindus believe that sex before marriage and adultery are both wrong because sex is only allowed in the householder stage of life and adultery brings bad karma.

Questions

b Do you think sex before marriage is wrong? Give two reasons for your point of view. **4**

c Choose one religion other than Christianity and explain why its followers are against sex outside marriage. **8**

d 'No religious person should ever have sex outside marriage.'

   i Do you agree? Give reasons for your opinion. **3**

   ii Give reasons why some people may disagree with you. **3**

Exam Tip

c 'Explain' means give reasons. To answer this question you should use two reasons against pre-marital sex and two reasons against adultery, and make each of them into a short paragraph. For tips on Quality of Written Communication, look at page 3.

Topic 3.3.4 Sikhism and sex outside marriage

Sikhs believe that sex outside marriage is wrong because:

- The Gurus did not have sex before marriage and all Sikhs should follow their examples.
- The Rahit Maryada says there should be no sex before marriage.
- Marriages are usually arranged by families. Having sex before marriage would make this more difficult.
- Adultery is breaking the marriage union and would be manmukh behaviour. It would make attaining mukti more difficult.
- Adultery is forbidden by the Rahit Maryada.
- All the human Gurus were faithful husbands who never committed adultery, and all Sikhs should follow their examples.
- Adultery is likely to harm the family. This should not be harmed as it is where children learn to be good Hindus.

The Beloved (God) has completed the union. The bride's mind has blossomed with the Beloved's name.

Lavan (wedding hymn)

Guru Gobind Singh with his wife. Why should Sikhs follow the example of the Gurus?

The Rahit Maryada says, 'A Sikh should respect another man's wife as he would his own mother, and another man's daughter as his own daughter.'

The bride should know no other man except her husband, so the Guru ordains ... Another person's property, another man's wife, talking ill of another, poisons one's life. Like the touch of a poisonous snake is the touch of another man's wife.

Advice on marriage from Guru Amar Das from the Sikh Marriage ceremony

Questions

b Do you think sex before marriage is wrong?
   Give two reasons for your point of view.   **4**
c Choose one religion other than Christianity and explain
   why its followers are against sex outside marriage.   **8**
d 'No religious person should ever have sex outside marriage.'
   i Do you agree? Give reasons for your opinion.   **3**
   ii Give reasons why some people may disagree with you.   **3**

Exam Tip

c 'Explain' means give reasons. To answer this question you should
   use two reasons against pre-marital sex and two reasons against
   adultery, and make each of them into a short paragraph. For tips
   on Quality of Written Communication, look at page 3.

SUMMARY

Sikhs believe that sex outside marriage is wrong. Sex before marriage is banned by the Rahit Maryada. Adultery breaks the sacred marriage union.

75

Topic 3.4 Christian attitudes to divorce

Thus the marriage bond has been established by God himself in such a way that a marriage concluded and consummated between baptised persons can never be dissolved.

Catechism of the Catholic Church 1640

The re-marriage of persons divorced from a living, lawful spouse contravenes the plan and law of God as taught by Christ.

Catechism of the Catholic Church 1665

For those who have taken their vows before God as Christians, there is no divorce. But most Baptists would acknowledge that human beings can make mistakes, and what appeared as a life-long relationship may eventually break down.

Statement by the Baptist Church in *What the Churches Say on Moral Issues*

There are different attitudes to divorce in Christianity:

1 The Catholic Church does not allow religious divorce or **re-marriage**. The only way a marriage between baptised Catholics can be ended is by the death of one of the partners.

The Catholic Church does allow civil divorce if that will be better for the children. But the couple are still married in the eyes of God and so cannot re-marry. Catholics have this attitude because:

- Jesus taught that divorce is wrong and Christians should follow his teachings.
- The couple have made a **covenant** with God which cannot be broken by any earthly power.
- The Catechism teaches that a marriage cannot be dissolved and so religious divorce is impossible.
- There can be no re-marriage as there can be no religious divorce. Re-marriage would be both bigamy (having two husbands/wives) and adultery.

However, if it can be proved that the marriage was never a true Christian marriage, Catholics can have an annulment which makes them free to re-marry.

Why do you think divorce is sometimes considered the lesser of two evils?

2 Most non-Catholic Churches think that divorce is wrong, but allow it if the marriage has broken down and allow divorced people to remarry. The divorced people are sometimes asked to promise that this time their marriage will be for life.

Non-Catholic Churches allow divorce because:

- Jesus allowed divorce in Matthew 19:9 for a partner's adultery.
- If a marriage has really broken down then the effects of the couple not divorcing would be a greater evil than the evil of divorce itself.
- If Christians repent and confess their sins they can be forgiven. This means a couple should have another chance at marriage if they are keen to make it work this time.
- These Churches believe it is better to divorce than live in hatred and quarrel all the time.

What type of Christian do you think might have drawn this cartoon?

Where a local church is in touch with one or both of the parties to a failed marriage, the offer of new life and the healing of memories is to be made. The possibility of new relationships and, where appropriate, a new marriage, is to be welcomed.

Statement by the Methodist Church in *What the Churches Say on Moral Issues*

When they were in the house again, the disciples asked Jesus about this. He answered 'Anyone who divorces his wife and marries another woman commits adultery against her. And if she divorces her husband and marries another man, she commits adultery.'

Mark 10:10–12

I tell you that anyone who divorces his wife, except for marital unfaithfulness, and marries another woman commits adultery.

Matthew 19:9

Questions

b Do you think divorce is better than an unhappy marriage? Give two reasons for your point of view. **4**

c Explain why some Christians allow divorce and some do not. **8**

d 'No Christian should ever get divorced.'

i Do you agree? Give reasons for your opinion. **3**

ii Give reasons why some people may disagree with you. **3**

Exam Tip

b You should already have thought about this, and you just have to give two reasons for your opinion. For example, if you agree with divorce you could use two reasons for non-Catholic Churches agreeing with divorce.

SUMMARY

- Catholics do not allow religious divorce and re-marriage because they believe the marriage vows cannot be broken.
- Other Christians disapprove of divorce, but allow religious divorce and re-marriage if the marriage has broken down because Christianity teaches forgiveness.

Topic 3.5.1 Islam and divorce

> O Prophet! When ye do divorce women, divorce them at their prescribed periods ... and fear God your Lord: and turn them not out of their houses.
>
> **Surah 65:1–2**

> Ibn Omer reported that the Messenger of Allah said, 'The most detestable of lawful things near Allah is divorce.'
>
> **Hadith recorded by Abu Daud**

> ... a woman is free to re-marry whoever she wishes (as long as she and her husband-to-be follow the terms of Islamic Law) and her former husband must not do anything to prevent her from doing so.
>
> **From *What does Islam say?* by I. Hewitt**

SUMMARY
- Most Muslims allow divorce because it is allowed by the Qur'an.
- Some Muslims do not allow divorce because Muhammad said God disapproves of it.

Divorce and re-marriage are allowed in Islam, but there are different attitudes.

1   Some Muslims would not divorce because:

- Muhammad is reported to have said that divorce is the most hated of lawful things. They follow what Muhammad said.
- Most marriages are arranged by families, so there is family pressure against divorce.
- Many Muslims believe they will be sent to hell if they harm their children, and divorce is likely to harm the children.
- The Qur'an teaches that families should try to rescue the marriage before they divorce.

2   Most Muslims believe that divorce should be allowed because:

- The Qur'an permits divorce and sets out the terms for custody of children and care for divorced wives.
- The Shari'ah permits divorce and has many laws about how divorce and re-marriage should operate.
- Most Muslims believe divorce is a lesser evil than forcing a couple to live in hatred and bitterness.
- Marriage is a contract in Islam and the contract says what is to happen if the couple divorce so divorce must be allowed.

Questions
b Do you think divorce is wrong? Give two reasons for your point of view.   **4**

c Choose one religion other than Christianity and explain why some of its followers allow divorce, but others are against it.   **8**

d 'No religious person should ever get divorced.'

   i Do you agree? Give reasons for your opinion.   **3**

   ii Give reasons why some people may disagree with you.   **3**

Exam Tip
c 'Explain' means give reasons. To answer this question you should use two reasons why some Muslims are against divorce and give two reasons why some Muslims allow divorce, and make each of them into a short paragraph. For tips on Quality of Written Communication, look at page 3.

Topic 3.5.2 Judaism and divorce

There are three different attitudes to divorce among Jewish people.

1   Some Jewish people believe that divorce is wrong because:

   • The Talmud teaches that divorce is an offence to God. They follow the Talmud teachings.
   • Children need to be brought up as good followers of Judaism for the faith to survive. Divorce may stop this.
   • Some rabbis have taught that divorce is wrong because of the harm it can cause.

2   Most Orthodox Jews allow divorce but only if the husband has a **get** from the **Bet Din** because:

   • The Torah has statements that permit divorce.
   • Marriage in Judaism is a contract that can be broken in certain circumstances.
   • The halakhah says that only men can apply to the Bet Din for a get.

3   Most **Reform Jews** allow divorce for both men and women because:

   • They believe that the Torah and halakhah need interpreting to fit modern life.
   • They believe that men and women should have equal rights in religion and also in divorce.
   • They believe divorce is a lesser evil than forcing a couple to live in hatred and bitterness.

> *If a man divorces his first wife, even the altar of the Temple sheds tears.*
>
> **The Talmud**

> *If a man marries a woman who becomes displeasing to him because he finds something indecent about her ... he writes her a certificate of divorce ...*
>
> **Deuteronomy 24:1**

Y.Y. Lichtenstein, Dayan of Rosh Bet Din in London.

Questions

b   Do you think divorce is wrong? Give two reasons for your point of view.   **4**
c   Choose one religion other than Christianity and explain why some of its followers allow divorce, but others are against it.   **8**
d   'No religious person should ever get divorced.'
   i   Do you agree? Give reasons for your opinion.   **3**
   ii   Give reasons why some people may disagree with you.   **3**

Exam Tip

c   'Explain' means give reasons. To answer this question you should use two reasons why some Jewish people are against divorce and give two reasons why some Jewish people allow divorce, and make each of them into a short paragraph. For tips on Quality of Written Communication, look at page 3.

SUMMARY

• Some Jewish people are against divorce because of the teachings of the Talmud and rabbis.
• Orthodox Jews allow divorce, but give special rights to men in divorce because of the Torah.
• Reform Jews allow divorce, but give equal divorce rights to women because they think the Torah should be brought up to date.

Topic 3.5.3 Hinduism and divorce

The Brahmin said, 'It is written in scripture, your majesty: "Protect your wife." When the wife is protected, the offspring are protected. For one's self is born in one's offspring; and when the offspring are protected, the self is protected. So she must be protected, your majesty. If she is not protected, the various classes will become commingled, and that will cause one's previous ancestors to fall from heaven.'

Shastra 5.3.6

Swaminarayan ... men avoid conversation with widows and women outside their families. Indeed a man is not to be alone in a room with a woman other than his wife, not even with a daughter.

From *A New Face of Hinduism* by R. Williams

SUMMARY

- Some Hindus do not allow divorce because they believe marriage is for life.
- Many Hindus allow divorce especially if the couple cannot have children because they think arguing and quarrelling in a marriage will give bad karma.

There are different attitudes to divorce among Hindus, but all Hindus believe divorced couples can re-marry.

1   Traditional Hindus believe that there should be no divorce, unless the couple are childless after fifteen years or if there is cruelty. They have this attitude because:

- It is the teaching of the Laws of Manu.
- Divorce is likely to harm families and so should be discouraged.
- Having children is part of your duty as a householder so childlessness is grounds for divorce.
- Violence in marriage is against ahimsa and so would be grounds for divorce.

2   Many other Hindus believe that divorce should be allowed if a marriage has broken down because:

- They regard the Laws of Manu as out of date.
- Some Gurus and **swamis** teach that divorce is acceptable for Hindus.
- Living in hatred and discord brings bad karma, so divorce would be needed for the soul to gain moksha.
- They believe divorce is a lesser evil than forcing a couple to live in hatred and bitterness.

Questions

b   Do you think divorce is wrong? Give two reasons for your point of view.   **4**

c   Choose one religion other than Christianity and explain why some of its followers allow divorce, but others are against it.   **8**

d   'No religious person should ever get divorced.'
   i   Do you agree? Give reasons for your opinion.   **3**
   ii   Give reasons why some people may disagree with you.   **3**

Exam Tip

c   'Explain' means give reasons. To answer this question you should use two reasons why some Hindus are against divorce and two reasons why some Hindus allow divorce, and make each of them into a short paragraph. For tips on Quality of Written Communication, look at page 3.

Topic 3.5.4 Sikhism and divorce

All Sikhs believe that marriage should be for life, but there are different attitudes to divorce.

1   Most Sikhs believe that there should be no divorce because:
    * Two souls are united in Sikh marriage, and they should not be split by divorce.
    * None of the Gurus divorced, and Sikhs should follow the example of the Gurus.
    * The Rahit Maryada disapproves of divorce and all good Sikhs should follow the guidance of the Rahit Maryada.
    * As Sikh marriages are often arranged, there are family pressures against divorce.

2   Some Sikhs believe that divorce should be allowed if a marriage has broken down because:
    * They follow the culture of the Punjab where divorce is common.
    * If a couple live in hatred and discord they will gather bad karma, but divorce might allow the soul to gain mukti.
    * They believe divorce is a lesser evil than forcing a couple to live in hatred and bitterness.

> *It is not unknown for a bride who is not pregnant on her first wedding anniversary to be sent home to her parents in disgrace and for a divorce to follow. This aspect of Punjabi or Indian culture should have no place among Sikhs.*
>
> **From *Teach Yourself Sikhism* by W. Owen Cole**

Uniting two families in marriage is a big argument against divorce in Sikhism.

Questions

b   Do you think divorce is wrong? Give two reasons for your point of view. **4**

c   Choose one religion other than Christianity and explain why some of its followers allow divorce, but others are against it. **8**

d   'No religious person should ever get divorced.'
    i   Do you agree? Give reasons for your opinion. **3**
    ii Give reasons why some people may disagree with you. **3**

Exam Tip

c   'Explain' means give reasons. To answer this question you should use two reasons why some Sikhs are against divorce and give two reasons why some Sikhs allow divorce, and make each of them into a short paragraph. For tips on Quality of Written Communication, look at page 3.

SUMMARY

* Some Sikhs believe there should be no divorce because marriage is for life and the Gurus did not divorce.
* Other Sikhs allow divorce because living in hatred will bring bad karma and prevent mukti.

Topic 3.6 Why family life is important for Christians

> The family is the community in which, from childhood, one can learn moral values, begin to honour God and make good use of freedom.
>
> **Catechism of the Catholic Church 2207**

Family life is important for Christians because:

- One of the main purposes of Christian marriage is to have children and bring them up in a Christian environment so that they become good Christians.
- Christianity teaches that the family was created by God as the basis of society and the only place for the upbringing of children.
- Christian teaching on divorce shows that the family is too important to be broken up by divorce.
- Without the family children would not learn the difference between right and wrong.
- The family is very important for Christianity to continue and grow as it is the family that brings children into the faith.

However, Jesus taught that there are more important things than the family which is why Catholic priests, nuns and monks leave their families to serve God.

> Children, obey your parents in the Lord, for this is right. 'Honour your father and mother' – which is the first commandment with a promise – 'that it may go well with you and that you may enjoy long life on the earth.'
> Fathers, do not exasperate your children; instead, bring them up in the training and instruction of the Lord.
>
> **Ephesians 6:1–4**

Questions

b Do you think families need a mother and father who are married? Give two reasons for your point of view. **4**

c Explain why family life is important for Christians. **8**

d 'Family life is more important for Christians than for non-religious people.'
   i Do you agree? Give reasons for your opinion. **3**
   ii Give reasons why some people may disagree with you. **3**

Exam Tip

c 'Explain' means give reasons. To answer this question you should use four of the above reasons for family life being important in Christianity, and make each of them into a short paragraph. For tips on Quality of Written Communication, look at page 3.

SUMMARY

Christians believe that the family is important because: it is taught in the Bible; Christian marriage services refer to bringing up a family as the main purposes of marriage; Christians believe that the family was created by God.

Topic 3.7.1 Islam and family life

Family life is important in Islam because:

- Muslim parents will be judged by God on how well they have brought up their children. If family life decides whether Muslims go to heaven, it must be very important.
- The Qur'an teaches that the family was created by God as the basic unit of society and as the only place in which children should be brought up.
- The Prophet Muhammad married and raised a family, so Muslims must marry and raise a family.
- Without the family children would not learn the difference between right and wrong.
- The family is very important for Islam to continue and grow as it is the family that brings children into the faith.

> Be careful of your duty to Allah and be fair and just to your children.
>
> **Hadith quoted by al'Bukhari**

Why is it important for Muslim parents to send their children to **madrasah**?

SUMMARY

Family life is important in Islam because the Qur'an says that the family is the basis of society and Muslims should follow the example of Muhammad who raised a family.

Questions

b Do you think family life is important? Give two reasons for your point of view. **4**

c Choose one religion other than Christianity and explain why family life is important in that religion. **8**

d 'Family life is more important for religious people than for non-religious people.'
  i Do you agree? Give reasons for your opinion. **3**
  ii Give reasons why some people may disagree with you. **3**

Exam Tip

d Remember to use the techniques for answering evaluation questions on page 9. Arguments for the statement would be the reasons in this topic. Arguments against would have to come from your class discussion or your own ideas. For example, if your own family is not religious, you could give examples of how important your family is to you and your parents.

Topic 3.7.2 Judaism and family life

> *Honour your father and your mother, so that you may live long in the land the Lord your God is giving you.*
>
> **Exodus 20:12**

The Chief Rabbi, Jonathan Sacks, who has held parenting seminars to help Jewish parents with their family life.

> *Today, the many elements in life which once held together are splitting apart. When we create a marriage, when we bring new life into the world, when we care for it, we are carrying out supreme religious acts. But how do we do it? To this, Judaism gave a simple answer, for it is above all a practical religion. The first and most important rule is: Make time for your children.*
>
> **Jonathan Sacks, Chief Rabbi**

SUMMARY

Family life is important in Judaism because the family is the only way of keeping Judaism alive and the Torah says all Jews should marry and raise a family.

Family life is important in Judaism because:

- Judaism teaches that the family was created by God as the basic unit of society and as the only place in which children should be brought up.

  - It is a mitzvot for Jewish people to marry and have children. Obeying the mitzvot is an essential part of being Jewish.
  - Only children of married Jewish parents are automatically Jewish. For this reason the family is very important for the continuation of the Jewish people and religion.
  - Without the family children would not learn the difference between right and wrong.
  - The family is the place where Shabbat is observed and the festivals are celebrated.
  - The importance of family life is commanded in the fifth of the Ten Commandments.

Questions

b Do you think family life is important? Give two reasons for your point of view. **4**

c Choose one religion other than Christianity and explain why family life is important in that religion. **8**

d 'Family life is more important for religious people than for non-religious people.'

   i Do you agree? Give reasons for your opinion. **3**

   ii Give reasons why some people may disagree with you. **3**

Exam Tip

d Remember to use the techniques for answering evaluation questions on page 9. Arguments for the statement would be the reasons in this topic. Arguments against would have to come from your class discussion or your own ideas. For example, if your own family is not religious, you could give examples of how important your family is to you and your parents.

Topic 3.7.3 Hinduism and family life

Family life is important in Hinduism because:

- Unless a Hindu performs his/her duties as a householder and raises a family, they will not achieve moksha. So the family is important as the way to reach nirvana.
- Hinduism teaches that the family was created by God as the basic unit of society and as the only place in which children should be brought up.
- Without the family children would not learn the difference between right and wrong.
- The family is very important for Hinduism to continue and grow as it is the family that brings children into the faith.
- The Hindu scriptures show the importance of Hindu family life and Hindus should follow the guidance of the scriptures.

> *Where the women are respected, there lives God. If the wife is obedient to the husband and the husband loves his wife; if the children obey the parents, and guests are entertained; if the family duty is performed and gifts are given to the needy, then there is heaven and nowhere else.*
>
> **The Laws of Manu**

Worshipping (puja) at the family **shrine** brings the family together.

Questions

b   Do you think family life is important? Give two reasons for your point of view.   **4**

c   Choose one religion other than Christianity and explain why family life is important in that religion.   **8**

d   'Family life is more important for religious people than for non-religious people.'
   i   Do you agree? Give reasons for your opinion.   **3**
   ii   Give reasons why some people may disagree with you.   **3**

Exam Tip

d   Remember to use the techniques for answering evaluation questions on page 9. Arguments for the statement would be the reasons in this topic. Arguments against would have to come from your class discussion or your own ideas. For example, if your own family is not religious, you could give examples of how important your family is to you and your parents.

SUMMARY

Family life is important in Hinduism because Hinduism teaches that the family is the basis of society and raising a family is part of the dharma of the householder stage of life.

Topic 3.7.4 Sikhism and family life

Family life is important in Sikhism because:

- Sikhism teaches that the family was created by God as the basic unit of society and as the only place in which children should be brought up.
- Sikhs believe that God is present in the home. The Guru Granth Sahib often refers to God as 'our father and mother'.
- The human Gurus married and had families, showing how important the family is.
- The Guru Granth Sahib teaches that family life is the highest form of life.
- Without the family children would not learn the difference between right and wrong.
- The family is very important for Sikhism to continue and grow as it is the family that brings children into the faith.

> *Family life is superior to the ascetic life (being a monk/holy man).*
>
> **Guru Granth Sahib 586**

> *It is the greatest sin to quarrel with parents who have given you birth and brought you up.*
>
> **Guru Granth Sahib 1200**

A Sikh family.

SUMMARY

The family is important in Sikhism because it was created by God to keep society together, and the family is the main way of keeping Sikhism alive.

Questions

b Do you think family life is important? Give two reasons for your point of view. **4**

c Choose one religion other than Christianity and explain why family life is important in that religion. **8**

d 'Family life is more important for religious people than for non-religious people.'
   i Do you agree? Give reasons for your opinion. **3**
   ii Give reasons why some people may disagree with you. **3**

Exam Tip

d Remember to use the techniques for answering evaluation questions on page 9. Arguments for the statement would be the reasons in this topic. Arguments against would have to come from your class discussion or your own ideas. For example, if your own family is not religious, you could give examples of how important your family is to you and your parents.

Topic 3.8 Christian attitudes to homosexuality

There are several attitudes to homosexuality in Christianity. The main ones are:

1. The Catholic attitude

The Catholic attitude is that being a homosexual is not a sin but homosexual sexual activity is a sin. The Catholic Church asks homosexuals to live without any sexual activity. It believes they will be helped to do this by the sacraments of the Church. The Church believes it is sinful to criticise homosexuals or attack their behaviour.

Catholics have this attitude because:

- The Bible condemns homosexual sexual activity.
- It is the tradition of the Church that any sexual activity should have the possibility of creating children.
- It is the teaching of the **Magisterium** which Catholics should believe.
- The Church teaches that people cannot help their sexual orientation, but they can control their sexual activity.

Christians, Jews and Muslims joined forces to campaign against the Gay Rights Bill in January 2007. Here a group of Christian protestors sing hymns.

It is necessary to distinguish between sexual orientation ... and indulging in sexual (genital) activity, homosexual or heterosexual. Neither a homosexual nor a heterosexual orientation leads inevitably to sexual activity. Furthermore, an individual's sexual orientation can be unclear, even complex. Also, it may vary over the years. Being a homosexual person is, then, neither morally good nor morally bad: it is homosexual genital acts that are morally wrong ... Homosexual people, as well as heterosexual people, can, and often do, give a fine example of friendship and the art of chaste loving.

A note on the teaching of the Catholic Church concerning homosexual people, Cardinal Hume 1995

The Church utterly condemns all forms of unjust discrimination, violence, harassment or abuse directed against people who are homosexual. Consequently, the Church teaches that homosexual people 'must be accepted with respect, compassion, and sensitivity'.

Cherishing Life, Catholic Bishops' Conference of England and Wales 2004

A civil partnership requires:

- both partners to provide reasonable maintenance for their civil partner and any children of the family
- civil partners to be assessed in the same way as husbands and wives for child support
- equal treatment for the purposes of life assurance, employment and pension benefits and recognition for immigration and nationality purposes.

The issue of homosexuality has caused major divisions in the Anglican Church (Churches in communion with the Church of England) since the Episcopal Church of the USA appointed an openly gay priest, Gene Robinson, as Bishop of New Hampshire. The Lambeth Conference declared in 1998 that homosexuals in a relationship should not be ordained as priests, and in 2004 called on the US Episcopal Church to repent for appointing an openly gay bishop.

Compiled from news stories

If all the gay people stayed away from church on a given Sunday, the Church of England would be close to shut down, between its organists, its clergy, its wardens ... it seems less than humble not to admit that.

Right Rev Gene Robinson interviewed in London, July 2007

2. The Evangelical Protestant attitude

Many Evangelical Protestants believe that homosexuality is a sin. They believe homosexuals can be changed by the power of the Holy Spirit. The reasons for this attitude are:

- The Bible says homosexuality is a sin and they believe that the Bible is the direct word of God.
- They believe that the **salvation** of Christ can remove all sins, including homosexuality.
- All the Churches have taught that homosexuality is wrong, even though some now say it is not.

However, the Evangelical Alliance has recently condemned homophobia and said churches should welcome homosexuals.

The Right Reverend Gene Robinson, who is the ninth bishop of New Hampshire in the Episcopal Church in the United States of America. He became the first openly gay bishop inside the wider Anglican Church in 2003. Should an openly gay man be appointed bishop?

3. The Liberal Protestant attitude

Many Liberal Protestants welcome homosexuals into the Church, and accept homosexual relationships. Some Liberal Protestants provide blessings for civil partnerships.

The reasons for this attitude are:

- They believe that the Bible texts condemning homosexuality show Jewish beliefs at the time rather than being the word of God.
- They feel that the major Christian belief in love and acceptance means that homosexuals must be accepted.
- Many believe that if homosexual Christians feel the Holy Spirit approves of their homosexuality, it must be true.
- They believe that Christians should be open and honest. So gay Christians should not be made to tell lies and pretend to be heterosexual.

Some Christian **ministers** and priests will give a church blessing for a civil partnership. Is this a good idea?

Questions

b Do you think homosexuals should have equal rights? Give two reasons for your point of view. **4**

c Explain why some Christians accept homosexuality and some do not. **8**

d 'No Christian should be homosexual.'
  i Do you agree? Give reasons for your opinion. **3**
  ii Give reasons why some people may disagree with you. **3**

Exam Tip

d Remember to use the techniques for answering evaluation questions on page 9. Arguments for the statement would be the reasons for the Evangelical Protestant view. Arguments against would be the reasons for the Liberal Protestant view.

SUMMARY

- Catholics believe there is nothing wrong with homosexual feelings or relationships as long as there is no sexual activity because this is the teaching of the Church.
- Evangelical Protestants believe that homosexuality is sinful because it is condemned in the Bible.
- Liberal Protestants believe that homosexuality is acceptable because it is natural and Christians should love and accept everyone.

Topic 3.9.1 Muslim attitudes to homosexuality

If two men among you are guilty of lewdness, punish them both. If they repent and amend, leave them alone; for God is oft-returning Most Merciful.

Surah 4:16

As Dr Zaki Badawi of the Muslim College, London, points out, the fact that homosexuality is incompatible with Islam does not mean gays or lesbians can be denied the right to call themselves Muslims, 'We can say that homosexuals are not good Muslims because they are practising an unacceptable sin but we cannot completely write them out of Islam. As long as they believe in Allah and the Messenger (peace be upon Him) none other than Allah has the authority to deny them their Islamic identity.'

1. The majority attitude

Most Muslims believe homosexuality is wrong because:
- Homosexuality is condemned by the Qur'an and the Qur'an is the final word of God.
- The Prophet Muhammad condemned homosexuality in several hadith, and Muslims should follow his teachings.
- God says in the Qur'an that marriage between a man and a woman is the only lawful form of sex.
- Islam teaches that any sexual activity should have the possibility of creating children.
- All Muslims should try to have a family, but homosexuals cannot.

2. The minority attitude

Some Muslims accept homosexuality because:
- They believe Islam is a religion of tolerance.
- They believe that God created and loves all people whatever their sexual orientation.
- They believe the scientific evidence means God must have made some people homosexual.

Questions
b Do you think religions should accept homosexuality? Give two reasons for your point of view. **4**
c Choose one religion other than Christianity and explain why some of its followers are against homosexuality, but others are not. **8**
d 'No religious person should ever be homosexual.'
    i Do you agree? Give reasons for your opinion. **3**
    ii Give reasons why some people may disagree with you. **3**

Exam Tip
c 'Explain' means give reasons. To answer this question you should use two of the above reasons for Muslims being against homosexuality, and two of the above reasons for some Muslims not being against homosexuality, and make each of them into a short paragraph. For tips on Quality of Written Communication, look at page 3.

SUMMARY
- Most Muslims believe homosexuality is wrong because it is condemned in the Qur'an and Shari'ah.
- A few Muslims believe that homosexuality should be accepted because it was created by God and Islam is a religion of peace and tolerance.

Topic 3.9.2 Jewish attitudes to homosexuality

There are two different attitudes to homosexuality in Judaism.

1 The Orthodox Jewish view is that being a homosexual is not a sin. However, homosexual sexual activity is a sin, as is homophobia. They have this attitude because:
- The Torah condemns homosexual activity and the Torah is the word of God.
- The Torah and Talmud declare that marriage between a man and a woman is the only lawful form of sex.
- Judaism teaches that any sexual activity should have the possibility of creating children.
- It is a mitzvot that Jewish adults should marry and raise a family which homosexuals cannot do.

2 The **Liberal** or Reform **Jews** see homosexuality as acceptable because:
- They believe that the Torah needs to be re-interpreted in the light of modern society.
- As scientists now believe that sexual orientation is natural, it must be given by God.
- They feel that labelling homosexuality as wrong leads to homophobia, which is linked to the evils of **racism**.

Rabbi Lionel Blue was the first openly gay Jewish rabbi in the UK.

Liberal Judaism encourages couples who choose to have a civil partnership to affirm their relationship with a religious ceremony. The ceremony might look very traditional, with the couple celebrating their commitment to one another under a **chuppah** *(the Jewish marriage canopy), or it might be a specially designed ceremony.*

Statement submitted to the *Report on Faiths and Homophobia,* **London 2007**

Questions

b Do you think religions should accept homosexuality? Give two reasons for your point of view. **4**
c Choose one religion other than Christianity and explain why some of its followers are against homosexuality, but others are not. **8**
d 'No religious person should ever be homosexual.'
   i Do you agree? Give reasons for your opinion. **3**
   ii Give reasons why some people may disagree with you. **3**

Exam Tip

c 'Explain' means give reasons. To answer this question you should use two of the above reasons for Jewish people being against homosexuality, and two of the above reasons for some Jewish people not being against homosexuality, and make each of them into a short paragraph. For tips on Quality of Written Communication, look at page 3.

SUMMARY

- Orthodox Jews believe homosexuality is wrong because it is condemned in the Torah and stops people from having children.
- Most Liberal/Reform Jews accept homosexuality because it is natural and Jewish people should respect others.

Topic 3.9.3 Hindu attitudes to homosexuality

A Hijra march in Bombay 2004 to protest against unfair treatment by the Indian authorities.

I am the power of those who are strong, when this power is free from passions and selfish desires. I am desire when this is pure, when this desire is not against righteousness.

Bhagavad Gita 7:11

When the tip of a hair is split into a hundred parts, and one of those parts further into a hundred parts – the individual soul, on the one hand, is the size of one such part, and, on the other, it partakes of infinity. It is neither a woman nor a man, nor even a hermaphrodite; it is ruled over by whatever body it obtains.

Svetasavatara Upanishad 5:9–10

SUMMARY

- Most Hindus believe that homosexuality is wrong because it stops people from fulfilling their duty as householders.
- Some Hindus accept homosexuality because it is natural and could be another way of finding moksha.

There are two attitudes to homosexuality in Hinduism.

1 Most Hindus disapprove of homosexuality and think it should not be practised by Hindus because:
   - The Laws of Manu only mention and approve of heterosexual sex.
   - All Hindus should pass through the householder stage of life. This means marriage and having a family – neither of which a homosexual can do.
   - Hinduism restricts sexual activity to the householder stage of marriage and family life.
   - As homosexuals cannot be householders, they will not be able to attain moksha.

2 Some Hindus believe that homosexuals should be treated the same as heterosexuals because:
   - There are sculptures and carvings of homosexual sex (both male and female) in old Hindu temples.
   - There are ways to achieve moksha other than being a householder.
   - There is a special **caste** of men called the Hijras who dress and behave as women to serve the mother goddess Parvati.
   - As scientists now believe that sexual orientation is natural, it must be given by God.

Questions

b Do you think religions should accept homosexuality? Give two reasons for your point of view. **4**

c Choose one religion other than Christianity and explain why some of its followers are against homosexuality, but others are not. **8**

d 'No religious person should ever be homosexual.'
   i Do you agree? Give reasons for your opinion. **3**
   ii Give reasons why some people may disagree with you. **3**

Exam Tip

c 'Explain' means give reasons. To answer this question you should use two of the above reasons for Hindus being against homosexuality, and two of the above reasons for some Hindus not being against homosexuality, and make each of them into a short paragraph. For tips on Quality of Written Communication, look at page 3.

Topic 3.9.4 Sikh attitudes to homosexuality

Neither the Guru Granth Sahib, nor the Rahit Maryada say anything about homosexuality, but there are two Sikh attitudes:

1   Many Sikhs still think that homosexuality is wrong because:
    - Sikhism expects all Sikhs to marry and raise a family.
    - The human Gurus married and had families, showing they were heterosexual. Sikhs should follow their examples.
    - Although the Gurus and the Rahit Maryada do not mention homosexuality, they do restrict sex to marriage.

2   Some Sikhs accept homosexuality and think homosexuals should be treated the same as anyone else because:
    - If homosexuality is wrong it would have been banned by the Guru Granth Sahib or the Rahit Maryada.
    - They believe that Sikh homosexuals should follow Sikh rules on marriage and be faithful to one partner.
    - As scientists now believe that sexual orientation is natural, it must be given by God.
    - Sikhs should respect all of God's creation and so homosexuals should be respected.

> *Basically, the relationship between men and women is very sacred and the ideal of joining two souls to realise God together. Homosexuality is not talked about in the scriptures and also in the lives of ten Gurus over a period of 200 years.*
>
> **Jasvinder Singh, ex–president of a gurdwara, answering the question, 'What stance does Sikhism take on the issue of homosexuality?'**

> *I am a gay man and was seeing another man who is a Sikh for a number of years. After much pressure, he ended our relationship as apparently it was against his religion. It is my belief that Sikhism needs to adapt to the twenty-first century and put up with everyone. How can they expect to be accepted if they are not willing to accept others? By way of a footnote, my ex is now married and by all accounts very unhappy.*
>
> **Martin, London
> Letter responding to a BBC debate on Sikhism**

Questions

b   Do you think religions should accept homosexuality? Give two reasons for your point of view. **4**

c   Choose one religion other than Christianity and explain why some of its followers are against homosexuality, but others are not. **8**

d   'No religious person should ever be homosexual.'
    i   Do you agree? Give reasons for your opinion. **3**
    ii Give reasons why some people may disagree with you. **3**

Exam Tip

c   'Explain' means give reasons. To answer this question you should use two of the above reasons for Sikhs being against homosexuality, and two of the above reasons for some Sikhs not being against homosexuality, and make each of them into a short paragraph. For tips on Quality of Written Communication, look at page 3.

SUMMARY

- Most Sikhs believe that homosexuality is wrong because it stops people from marrying and raising a family.
- Some Sikhs accept homosexuality because it is natural and is not mentioned in the Sikh scriptures.

Topic 3.10 Different Christian attitudes to contraception

KEY WORD

Contraception – intentionally preventing pregnancy from occurring.

Throughout history people have tried to control the number of children that they have. This was to provide a better standard of living for the family and to help the mother's health.

Condoms were developed in the nineteenth century but the contraceptive pill has became the main form of artificial **contraception**. Since the rise of AIDS/HIV, condoms have been recommended for safe sex.

There are two main attitudes to contraception among Christians.

1. The Catholic attitude

The Catholic Church has always taught responsible parenthood. This involves deciding on how many children to have and when to have them. However, the Catholic way to achieve this is through using natural family planning rather than artificial methods of contraception. Natural family planning means restricting sex to when the woman is least fertile. Catholics believe this because:

In July 1987, at a conference on responsible procreation, Pope John Paul II reminded Christians attending that there is an 'inseparable connection, willed by God and unable to be broken by man ... between the two meanings of the conjugal act (married sexual act); the unitive and the procreative.'

The methods of birth regulation based on self-observation and the use of infertile periods ... respect the bodies of the spouses, encourage tenderness between them ... In contrast, 'every action which ... proposes ... to render procreation impossible' is ... evil.

Catechism of the Catholic Church 2370

- Pope Pius XI condemned all forms of artificial contraception.
- Pope Pius XII declared that Catholics could use natural methods of contraception.
- Pope Paul VI stated that the only allowable forms of contraception are natural methods, and this teaching has been confirmed in the Catechism of the Catholic Church.

Pope Pius XI.

- The Church teaches that all sex should be unitive (bringing the couple together) and creative (bringing new life).
- Some contraceptives bring about a very early abortion (abortifacient).
- The Catholic Church believes artificial contraception leads to **promiscuity**, broken families, divorce and sexually transmitted diseases.

2. The attitude of non-Catholic Christians

Almost all non-Catholic Christians believe that all forms of contraception are permissible because:

- Christianity is about love and justice, and contraception improves women's health and raises the standard of living.
- God created sex for enjoyment and to strengthen marriage which is more likely without the risk of pregnancy.
- There is nothing in the Bible that forbids the use of contraception.
- In 1930, the Lambeth Conference of the worldwide Anglican Communion (**Church of England**) said Christians could use contraception to limit family size.
- They believe that using condoms is the best way to combat the spread of AIDS/HIV.

Contraception is seen as a gift from medical science ... Choosing not to have or space families is morally defensible, considering the needs of the world, population size and family responsibility. However, those contraceptives that have an abortifacient function (for example, IUD and various pills) are considered to take human life and should be avoided.

Statement by the Baptist Church in *What the Churches Say*

Questions

b Do you think contraception should be used? Give two reasons for your point of view. **4**

c Explain why some Christians allow artificial methods of contraception and some do not. **8**

d 'Christians should never use contraceptives.'
  i Do you agree? Give reasons for your opinion. **3**
  ii Give reasons why some people may disagree with you. **3**

Exam Tip

b You should already have thought about this, and you just have to give two reasons for your opinion. For example, if you agree with contraception, you could use two reasons for non-Catholic Churches agreeing with contraception.

SUMMARY

The Catholic Church teaches that using artificial methods of contraception to stop a baby being conceived is wrong. God gave sex in order to create children. Other Christians allow the use of contraception because they believe God gave sex to strengthen a married relationship.

Topic 3.11.1 Muslim attitudes to contraception

A Muslim family.

> If Allah wishes to create a child, you cannot prevent it.
>
> **Hadith reported by four authorities**

> Contraception is not like abortion. Abortion is a crime against an existing being.
>
> **Imam Al-Ghazzali**

SUMMARY

- Some Muslims are against the use of contraceptives because they believe God created sex for procreation.
- Other Muslims agree with contraception because the Prophet and law schools do.

All Muslims believe they should have children, but there are different attitudes as to whether contraception can be used to limit the number of children.

1 Some Muslims believe that contraception should not be used at all because:
   - They believe the Qur'an's command, 'You should not kill your children for fear of want' means a ban on contraception.
   - They believe that God created sex for having children.
   - They are opposed to abortion and so would not allow any contraceptives that acted as abortifacients.
   - They believe it is the duty of Muslims to have large families.

2 Some Muslims believe that it is permitted for Muslims to use contraception to limit the number of children because:
   - There are several hadith which record that the Prophet permitted the use of **coitus interruptus** as a means of contraception.
   - The Qur'an says God does not place extra burdens on his followers, and contraception stops extra burdens.
   - If pregnancy risks a mother's health, contraception must be allowed because Islam puts the mother's life first.
   - Muslim lawyers agree that contraception is different from abortion and so should be permitted.

Questions

b Do you think religions should allow their followers to use contraceptives? Give two reasons for your point of view. **4**

c Choose one religion other than Christianity and explain why some of its followers accept any form of contraception and some do not. **8**

d 'No religious person should use artificial methods of contraception.'
   i Do you agree? Give reasons for your opinion. **3**
   ii Give reasons why some people may disagree with you. **3**

Exam Tip

d Remember to use the techniques for answering evaluation questions on page 9. Arguments for the statement would be the reasons for the traditional Muslim view. Arguments against would be the reasons for the Liberal Muslim view.

Topic 3.11.2 Jewish attitudes to contraception

There are three different attitudes to contraception in Judaism:

1 Very Orthodox Jews (the Ultra Orthodox) do not approve of any form of artificial contraception, unless the mother's health is at risk because:
   - They believe God's command that Jewish people should be fruitful means they should have large families.
   - The Torah says the male sperm is sacred and not to be killed.
   - Many rabbis teach that God created sex for having children.

2 Orthodox Jews allow women to use contraception after a couple has had two children because:
   - Torah, Talmud and the rabbis teach that the health of the mother should come first.
   - Contraceptives for women do not kill the male seed.
   - It is a mitzvot to have a family and having two children obeys this.
   - Use of condoms to protect against HIV has to be approved by the rabbi.

3 The Liberal/Reform Jews believe decisions about contraception are up to the couple because:
   - God expects people to use intelligence and technology to make life better.
   - They believe the Torah needs updating and contraception should be available to men and women.
   - It is better to use contraception than bring unwanted children into the world.

> *Then God blessed Noah and his sons, saying to them, 'Be fruitful and increase in number and fill the earth.'*
>
> **Genesis 9:1**

SUMMARY

- Ultra Orthodox Jews do not allow contraception because they believe God wants them to have large families.
- Orthodox Jews allow only female contraception because the Torah says the male seed is sacred.
- Liberal/Reform Jews allow any form of contraception because they believe the Torah should be brought up to date.

Exam Tip

c Remember to use the techniques for answering evaluation questions on page 9. Arguments for the statement would be the reasons for the Orthodox view. Arguments against would be the reasons for the Liberal/Reform view.

Questions

b Do you think religions should allow their followers to use contraceptives? Give two reasons for your point of view. **4**

c Choose one religion other than Christianity and explain why some of its followers accept any form of contraception and some do not. **8**

d 'No religious person should use artificial methods of contraception.'
   i   Do you agree? Give reasons for your opinion. **3**
   ii Give reasons why some people may disagree with you. **3**

Topic 3.11.3 Hindu attitudes to contraception

> *When a man deposits the semen in a woman … it becomes one with the woman's body as if it were part of her own body.*
>
> **Aitareya Upanishad 2:2**

Why would many Hindus take notice of this poster?

SUMMARY

- Most Hindus believe in contraception because it does not affect the soul and it helps the population not to exceed the food supply.
- Some Hindus only accept contraceptives which do not kill sperm or eggs because of their beliefs in ahimsa.
- A few Hindus are against all forms of contraception because they believe it is the duty of a householder to have a large family.

Exam Tip

d Remember to use the techniques for answering evaluation questions on page 9. Arguments for the statement would be the reasons for the traditional Hindu view. Arguments against would be the reasons for the Liberal Hindu view.

There are three attitudes to contraception in Hinduism:

1 Most Hindus believe that all forms of contraception are good because they believe:

- The householder stage of life should be about fulfilling one's dharma, not struggling to cope with a large family.
- The soul cannot be affected by contraception, as there is no soul before conception.
- Humans have a duty to make sure that the population does not exceed the food supply.
- Contraception does not involve violence to a living thing and so it is not against ahimsa.

2 Some Hindus only accept certain forms of contraception, such as the pill and sterilisation because:

- They believe that contraceptives that kill either sperm or eggs are against ahimsa.
- They are against abortion and so cannot accept abortifacient contraceptives.

3 A few Hindus are against any form of contraception because:

- They believe that large families are part of the householder stage of life.
- They believe that sex must involve the possibility of children to fulfil dharma.
- They believe strongly in ahimsa and think that any contraceptives that kill either sperm or eggs or bring an early abortion are against ahimsa.

Questions

b Do you think religions should allow their followers to use contraceptives? Give two reasons for your point of view. **4**

c Choose one religion other than Christianity and explain why some of its followers accept any form of contraception and some do not. **8**

d 'No religious person should use artificial methods of contraception.'

   i Do you agree? Give reasons for your opinion. **3**

   ii Give reasons why some people may disagree with you. **3**

Topic 3.11.4 Sikh attitudes to contraception

There are different attitudes to contraception among Sikhs.

A child is born when it pleases God.
Guru Granth Sahib 921

1   Some Sikhs think that it is wrong to use contraceptives because they believe:
   • God gave sex to humans to have children.
   • Contraception is killing life and that is banned in the Guru Granth Sahib.
   • Sikhs should follow the example of the human Gurus who had large families.

2   Most Sikhs believe contraceptives can be used to limit family size after two children because:
   • They believe life does not begin until the moment of conception.
   • The Guru Granth Sahib says that God does not intend humans to suffer and contraception stops suffering.
   • Having a small family is still following the examples of the Gurus.

3   Some Sikhs think married Sikhs can use any form of contraception because:
   • Contraception is not mentioned in the Guru Granth Sahib or the Rahit Maryada.
   • The teaching of the Guru Granth Sahib on God not wanting humans to suffer means that they should only have have wanted children.

Questions
b Do you think religions should allow their followers to use contraceptives? Give two reasons for your point of view.   **4**
c Choose one religion other than Christianity and explain why some of its followers accept any form of contraception and some do not.   **8**
d 'No religious person should use artificial methods of contraception.'
   i   Do you agree? Give reasons for your opinion.   **3**
   ii Give reasons why some people may disagree with you.   **3**

Exam Tip
d Remember to use the techniques for answering evaluation questions on page 9. Arguments for the statement would be the reasons for the traditional Sikh view. Arguments against would be the reasons for the Liberal Sikh view.

SUMMARY
• Some Sikhs believe contraception is wrong because all sex should allow for the procreation of life.
• Most Sikhs believe contraception can be used to limit family size after two children.
• Some Sikhs believe a married couple can use contraception because it is not mentioned in the Sikh holy book.

How to answer exam questions

Question A What is a re-constituted family?   2 marks

Where two sets of children (step-brothers and sisters) become one family when their divorced parents marry each other.

Question B Do you think contraception should be used?
Give two reasons for your point of view.   4 marks

Yes I do because there is nothing in the Bible that forbids the use of contraception so Christians can use it. Also contraception makes families happier. The mother has time for the children because she is not pregnant all the time, and the family will have more money.

Question C Choose one religion other than Christianity and explain why family life is important in that religion.   8 marks

Family life is important in Islam because Islam teaches that the family was created by God to keep society together. If the family was created by God, it must be important.

  Muslims believe that the family is the only way approved by God to bring up children. Therefore the family must be important because society needs children.

  Muslims also believe the family is important because it is in the family that children learn about Islam and are taught how to follow the Five Pillars, by praying at home, giving zakah, fasting in Ramadan and learning about hajj.

  Perhaps the main reason why the family is important in Islam is because all Muslims try to follow the example of the Prophet Muhammad. Muhammad was married and had a family and so it is very important for Muslims also to marry and have a family.

Question D 'A religious wedding ceremony helps to make a marriage work.'

  i Do you agree? Give reasons for your opinion.   3 marks

  ii Give reasons why some people may disagree with you.   3 marks

i I do not agree because I believe that love is what makes a marriage work. It seems to me that just as many people who have a religious wedding ceremony get divorced as those who do not have a religious wedding ceremony. If you make a promise to stay with someone you love, you will not break that promise whether you make it to God as well or not. People who have affairs do not seem to think, 'God will punish me for this'. So I disagree with the statement.

ii Many Christians would disagree with me. They believe that a religious wedding ceremony helps to make a marriage work because the couple make promises to God to stay together and breaking that promise would be like lying to God. Also at the ceremony prayers are said by a priest asking God's blessing and so God will be helping to make the marriage work. Finally they get advice at the ceremony from the Bible and the priest about how to make the marriage work.

QUESTION A
A high mark answer because it gives a correct definition.

QUESTION B
A high mark answer because an opinion is backed up by two developed reasons.

QUESTION C
A high mark answer because four reasons for family life being important in Islam are developed. A formal style of English is used and there is good use of specialist vocabulary – Five Pillars, prayer, zakah, Ramadan, hajj, example of the Prophet Muhammad.

QUESTION D
A high mark answer because it states the candidate's own opinion and backs it up with three clear reasons for thinking that a religious ceremony does not help to make a marriage work. It then gives three reasons for Christians disagreeing and believing that a religious ceremony does help to make a marriage work.

Section 4 Religion and community cohesion

Introduction

This section of the examination specification requires you to look at issues surrounding the roles of men and women, racial harmony, religious harmony and the media and community cohesion.

Roles of men and women

You will need to understand the effects of, and give reasons for your own opinion about:

- how and why attitudes to the roles of men and women have changed in the United Kingdom
- different Christian attitudes to equal rights for women in religion
- different attitudes to equal rights for women in religion in one religion other than Christianity.

Racial harmony

You will need to understand the effects of, and give reasons for your own opinion about:

- the nature of the United Kingdom as a multi-ethnic society
- government action to promote community cohesion in the United Kingdom
- why Christians should help to promote racial harmony
- why the followers of one religion other than Christianity should help to promote racial harmony.

Religious harmony

You will need to understand the effects of, and give reasons for your own opinion about:

- the United Kingdom as a multi-faith society
- issues raised for religion by a multi-faith society
- ways in which religions work to promote community cohesion in the United Kingdom.

The media and community cohesion

You will need to understand the effects of, and give reasons for your own opinion about how an issue from religion and community cohesion has been presented in one form of the media and whether the treatment was fair to religious beliefs and religious people.

Topic 4.1 How and why attitudes to the roles of men and women have changed in the United Kingdom

Women make up 84 per cent of employees in personal services (care assistants, child minders, hairdressers, etc).

Men make up 66 per cent of managers, senior officials, professionals.

Source: Census 2001

Statistics

The gender pay gap (the difference between men's and women's hourly pay) is narrowing:

1986	26 per cent
2002	19 per cent
2007	12.6 per cent

Average minutes spent per day

Activity	Men	Women
Cooking	27	54
Cleaning	13	47
Laundry	4	18
Caring for children	22	42

Source: ONS

How attitudes have changed

During the second half of the nineteenth century, it became the accepted view that married women should stay at home and look after the children.

However, women began to fight to have equal rights with men. The Married Women's Property Act 1882 allowed married women to keep their property separate from their husband's. The Local Government Act gave women the right to stand as councillors. However, it was not until 1928 that women were given equal voting rights and could become MPs.

Equal rights in employment did not arrive until the Equal Pay Act of 1970 gave women the right to the same pay as men for the same job. In 1975, the Sex Discrimination Act made it illegal to discriminate in employment on grounds of gender or whether someone is married.

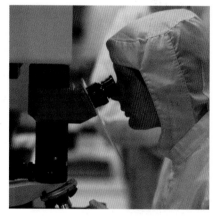

A female technician. How does this image show changing attitudes to the role of women?

Attitudes to the roles of men and women have been slower to change. Although in 2008, only 17 per cent of men agreed that 'a man's job is to earn money, a woman's job is to look after the home and family', who actually does the work around the home has not changed as much.

- 77 per cent of people living with partners in 2008 said that the woman always does the laundry
- 68 per cent of women still think they do all the housework
- though only 54 per cent of men think that their partner does all the housework
  (Source: British Social Attitudes Report January 2008).

Figures on salaries, promotion prospects, care of children and elderly relatives, etc., show that there is still a way to go before men and women have complete equality in the UK.

Why might this have surprised people in 1943?

Why attitudes have changed

- During the First and Second World Wars, women had to take on many of the jobs previously done by men and did these jobs just as well as men.
- The development of equal rights for women in other countries made it difficult to claim they were not needed in the UK.
- The success of women as councillors and women's work in health and social care showed that women were the equals of men in these areas.
- The work of the suffragette movement to gain equal rights for women showed that women were no longer prepared to be treated as second class citizens.
- Social and industrial developments in the 1950s and 1960s led the need for more women workers.
- The UN Declaration of Human Rights and the development of the Feminist Movement meant equal rights had to be accepted.
- The Labour governments of 1964–70 and 1974–79 were dedicated to equal rights for women.

Everyone is entitled to all the rights and freedoms set forth in this Declaration, without distinction of any kind, such as race, colour, sex, language, religion, political or other opinion, national or social origin, property, birth or other status.

Article 2 of the UN Declaration of Human Rights

Questions

b Do you think men should share housework with women? Give two reasons for your point of view. **4**

c Explain how attitudes to the roles of men and women have changed. **8**

d 'Men and women should have equal roles in life.'
  i Do you agree? Give reasons for your opinion. **3**
  ii Give reasons why some people may disagree with you. **3**

Exam Tip

c 'Explain' means give reasons. To answer this question you should use four changes from this topic, beginning with what the attitude used to be and explaining how it has changed. Your answer should be four short paragraphs. For tips on Quality of Written Communication, look at page 3.

SUMMARY

Attitudes to the roles of men and women have changed greatly. Women now have equal rights and men and women are expected to share roles in the home. Attitudes have changed because of the Feminist Movement, social and industrial changes and the effects of the World Wars.

Topic 4.2 Different Christian attitudes to equal rights for women in religion

> *I do not permit a woman to teach or to have authority over a man; she must be silent. For Adam was formed first, then Eve. And Adam was not the one deceived; it was woman who was deceived and became a sinner.*
>
> **1 Timothy 2:12–14**

> *A wife is to submit graciously to the servant leadership of her husband even as the Church willingly submits to the leadership of Christ ... she, being in the image of God, as is her husband and thus equal to him, has the God-given responsibility to respect her husband and to serve as his helper.*
>
> **Statement by the Southern Baptist Convention of the USA, June 1998**

> *You are all sons of God through faith in Christ Jesus, for all of you who were baptised into Christ have clothed yourselves with Christ. There is neither Jew nor Greek, slave nor free, male nor female, for you are all one in Christ Jesus.*
>
> **Galatians 3:26–28**

There are different attitudes to equal rights for women in religion in Christianity:

1. The traditional attitude of Protestant Christianity

Many Evangelical Protestants teach that men and women have separate and different roles and so cannot have equal rights in religion. Women should not speak in church and only men can be church leaders and teachers.

They have this attitude because:

- In the Bible, St Paul teaches that women should not teach or speak in church.
- St Paul also uses the story of Adam and Eve in Genesis to show that men have been given more rights by God because Adam was created first.
- Although Jesus had women followers, he chose only men as his twelve **apostles**.

Traditional Protestant Christians believe women should grow their hair long and keep their heads covered as instructed in I Corinthians 11:3–10.

- It has always been the tradition of the Church that only men should be leaders in the Church.

2. The modern attitude of Protestant Christianity

Many Protestant Churches (e.g. Church of England, **Methodist**, **United Reformed Church (URC)**, Baptist) give men and women equal rights, and have women ministers and priests, because:

- The creation story in Genesis 1 says that God created male and female at the same time in his image and therefore of equal status.
- In some of his letters, Paul teaches that men and women are equal in Christ.
- There is evidence from the Gospels that Jesus treated women as his equals. For example, he had women

disciples who stayed with him at the cross unlike the male disciples who ran away. After his resurrection, Jesus appeared first to his women disciples.

- There is some evidence that there were women priests in the early Church.

3. Catholic attitudes to the roles of men and women

The Catholic Church teaches that men and women should have equal rights in society and in religion except that they cannot be part of the ordained ministry (deacons, priests and bishops). They have this attitude because:

- The creation story in Genesis 1 says that God created male and female at the same time in his image and therefore of equal status.
- It is the teaching of the Catholic Catechism that men and women are equal, and should have equal rights in life and society.
- The Third World Synod of Bishops in 1971 called for women to take part in the life of society and of the Church.
- Only men can be priests because the apostles were all men, and priests and bishops are successors of the apostles.
- Only men can be priests because Jesus was a man and the priest represents Jesus in the **Mass**.

> *The Lord Jesus chose men to form the college of the twelve apostles, and the apostles did the same when they chose collaborators to succeed them in their ministry ... for this reason, the ordination of women is impossible.*
>
> **Catechism of the Catholic Church 1577**

Should women be allowed to become bishops?

Questions

b Do you think women should have equal rights in religion? Give two reasons for your point of view. **4**

c Explain why some Christians give equal roles to women in religion and some do not. **8**

d 'Women should have equal roles in Christianity.'
  i Do you agree? Give reasons for your opinion. **3**
  ii Give reasons why some people may disagree with you. **3**

Exam Tip

b You should already have thought about this, and you just have to give two reasons for your opinion. For example, if you agree with equal rights for women in religion you could use two reasons for modern Protestants agreeing with them.

SUMMARY

- Traditional Protestants believe only men should be religious leaders because this is what the Bible teaches.
- Liberal Protestants believe men and women have equal roles in religion because Jesus had women disciples.
- Catholics believe men and women should have equal roles, but only men can become priests because Jesus was a man.

Topic 4.3.1 Islam and equal rights for women in religion

There are different attitudes to equal rights for women in religion among Muslims:

> *Women have the same rights in relation to their husbands as are expected in all decency of them; while men stand a step above them.*
>
> **Surah 2:228**

1. The traditional attitude

Some Muslims believe that men and women should have different roles in life and religion, and therefore they should have different rights. They believe women should perform their religious duties (except hajj) in the home and men should worship God in the **mosque** with their sons and lead the religion.

> *Men are the ones who support women since God has given some persons advantages over others.*
>
> **Surah 4:34**

They have this attitude because:

- The Qur'an teaches that men should support women because God has made men physically stronger.
- The Qur'an teaches that women have been created to bear children and men to provide for them.
- The Qur'an teaches that men need more money than women to be the family providers.

Do you think these young women in Damascus have a traditional or modern attitude?

- It is traditional for only men to attend the mosque and to be **imams**.

2. The modern attitude

Some Muslims believe that men and women should have completely equal rights in religion and education and a few would accept women religious leaders.

They have this attitude because:

- The Qur'an teaches that men and women are equal in religion and education.
- There is evidence that Muhammad encouraged both men and women to worship in the mosque.
- There were women religious leaders during the early stages of Islam.
- They have been affected by the non-religious arguments for equal rights for women.

Many British Muslims mix these two attitudes and agree with women having equal rights in everything except religion.

> *Whoever works deeds of righteousness, man or woman ... verily to him will We give a new life.*
>
> **Surah 16:97**

> *The search for knowledge is a duty for every Muslim, male or female.*
>
> **Hadith quoted by al'Bukhari**

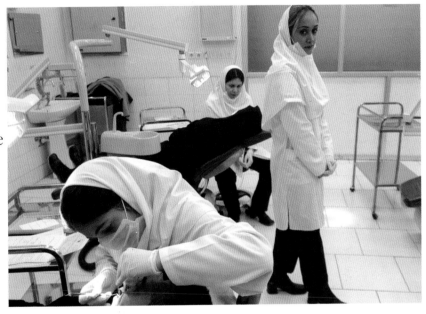

Female dentistry students at Tehran University mix modern and traditional attitudes.

Questions

b Choose one religion other than Christianity. Do you think women should have equal roles in this religion? Give two reasons for your point of view. **4**

c Choose one religion other than Christianity and explain why some followers give equal roles to women in religion and some do not. **8**

d 'Women should have the same rights as men in religion.'

  i Do you agree? Give reasons for your opinion. **3**

  ii Give reasons why some people may disagree with you. **3**

Exam Tip

d Remember to use the techniques for answering evaluation questions on page 9. Arguments for the statement would be the reasons for the modern attitude in this topic. Arguments against would be the reasons for the traditional attitude in this topic.

SUMMARY

- Traditional Muslims believe that men and women should have different roles in religion because of tradition and the teachings of the Qur'an.
- Modern Muslims believe that men and women should have equal roles in religion because of the teachings of the Qur'an and the example of the Prophet.

Topic 4.3.2 Judaism and equal rights for women in religion

> To the woman he said, 'I will greatly increase your pain in childbearing; with pain you will give birth to children. Your desire will be for your husband and he will rule over you.
>
> **Genesis 3:16**

There are different attitudes to equal rights for women in religion in Judaism:

1. The Orthodox attitude

Most Orthodox Jews give equal rights to women in all areas of life except religion where they believe that men and women have different roles. It is the role of women to keep a kosher home and sit separately from the men in the **synagogue**. It is the role of men to perform the ritual prayers every day and make sure the synagogue provides all the worship and education needed. Orthodox Jewish women cannot be religious leaders or rabbis.

They have this attitude because:

- It is the teaching of the Torah, Talmud and rabbis.
- The mitzvot only apply to men therefore women cannot have the same rights in religion as men.
- Women cannot form a **minyan** and so cannot have equal rights with men in the synagogue.
- Women cannot be witnesses in a Bet Din court and so cannot have equal rights with men in the religious laws of Judaism.

How can you tell this is an Orthodox synagogue?

2. The Liberal/Reform attitude

In Liberal/Reform and Progressive Judaism, men and women have completely equal rights and there are women rabbis.

They have this attitude because:

- The creation story in Genesis 1 says that God created male and female at the same time and of equal status.
- They believe that the Torah needs to be interpreted for today's world, and those parts of the Torah denying equal rights to women should no longer apply.
- They believe that to deny equal rights to women in religion is the same as saying that God prefers men to women.
- They believe that Judaism should relate to attitudes in the modern world and so should accept equal rights for women.

How can you tell this is not an Orthodox synagogue?

Times have changed. Women do not marry young, do not have many children. They lead their own lives as single, married or divorced women, and it is up to Reform Judaism to re-interpret the Torah in the light of these changes.

The First Jewish Catalogue

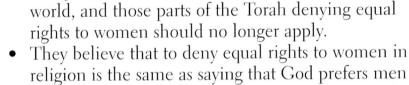

Questions

b Choose one religion other than Christianity. Do you think women should have equal roles in this religion? Give two reasons for your point of view. **4**

c Choose one religion other than Christianity and explain why some followers give equal roles to women in religion and some do not. **8**

d 'Women should have the same rights as men in religion.'
  i Do you agree? Give reasons for your opinion. **3**
  ii Give reasons why some people may disagree with you. **3**

Exam Tip

d Remember to use the techniques for answering evaluation questions on page 9. Arguments for the statement would be the reasons for the Liberal/Reform attitude in this topic. Arguments against would be the reasons for the Orthodox attitude in this topic.

SUMMARY

- Orthodox Jews believe that men and women are equal but have different roles in religion because it is the teaching of the Torah.
- Reform Jews believe that men and women have completely equal roles in religion and accept women as rabbis because God created men and women with equal status.

Topic 4.3.3 Hinduism and equal rights for women in religion

There are different attitudes to equal rights for women in religion in Hinduism:

1. The traditional attitude

Some Hindus believe that men and women have different roles and so cannot have equal rights in religion. They do not allow women to be priests or religious leaders because:

- It is the teaching of the shruti scriptures.
- It is the teaching of the Laws of Manu which must be followed to fulfil your dharma and achieve moksha.
- It is the tradition for the householder stage of life which all Hindus must complete.
- It is part of Indian culture which traditional Hindus regard as part of Hinduism.

> The father protects the woman in childhood, the husband protects her in youth, the children protect her in old age, a woman should never be independent.
>
> **Laws of Manu**

> Go to your husband's home and take charge of it. Occupy the main position and carry out all the activities connected with the home. Here may you have children and protect your happiness.
>
> **Hindu Marriage service**

Why do you think some Hindus see worship in the home as a woman's role in religion?

2. The modern attitude

Some Hindus (such as **Iskcon** and the **Virashaivas**) give women equal rights in both life and religion. They have women religious leaders because:

An Indian woman taking a break from cleaning the statue that commemorates the Salt March of 1930 in which both men and women marched against British rule.

- They believe that all souls are actually or potentially part of the divine and so are equal.
- They believe that even the shruti scriptures need interpreting for today's world.
- They believe that the Laws of Manu were intended for a different time and society.
- They believe there are other ways to gain moksha than following the traditional ashramahs.

Some modern Hindus (such as the **Swaminarayan**) would say that men and women should have equal rights in life, but they do not give women equal rights in religion.

Women from various backgrounds responded enthusiastically to Gandhi's call to participate in the national struggle for freedom (from British rule) ... It had important implications. Both men and women became equal partners in a common cause. Women were able to come out into the open and thus break the barriers of caste and sex. Women availed themselves of educational opportunities and qualified for professions such as law, medicine, teaching, social work and the like.

From *Themes and Issues in Hinduism*, edited by P. Bowen

Questions

b Choose one religion other than Christianity. Do you think women should have equal roles in this religion? Give two reasons for your point of view. **4**

c Choose one religion other than Christianity and explain why some followers give equal roles to women in religion and some do not. **8**

d 'Women should have the same rights as men in religion.'
  i Do you agree? Give reasons for your opinion. **3**
  ii Give reasons why some people may disagree with you. **3**

Exam Tip

d Remember to use the techniques for answering evaluation questions on page 9. Arguments for the statement would be the reasons for the modern attitude in this topic. Arguments against would be the reasons for the traditional attitude in this topic.

SUMMARY

- Traditional Hindus teach that men and women have different roles in religion because of the Laws of Manu.
- Modern Hindus believe that men and women should have equal roles in religion because all souls are part of the divine and so are equal.

Topic 4.3.4 Sikhism and equal rights for women in religion

There are different attitudes to equal rights for women in religion in Sikhism:

> *The wise and beauteous Being is neither man nor woman nor bird.*
>
> **Guru Granth Sahib**

> *You are our mother and father, we are your children.*
>
> **Guru Granth Sahib**

1. The religious attitude

Sikhism teaches the complete equality of men and women, and so most Sikhs believe that women should have equal rights in religion because:

- **Guru Nanak** taught that male and female are to be seen as two halves of a whole who therefore have equal rights.
- Equal rights for women was the teaching of all the other Gurus. For example, **Guru Amar Das** appointed women as Sikh preachers and Mati Sahib Kaur mixed the **amrit** for the first **initiation ceremony**.
- The Guru Granth Sahib teaches that God is neither male nor female.
- The Guru Granth Sahib teaches that men and women have so much in common that they must be treated the same.

Which Sikh attitude to women is shown in this **langar**?

2. The cultural attitude

Some Sikhs believe that men and women should have different roles and so cannot have equal rights in religion. They believe that women should look after the home and children, not be religious leaders because:

- Most Sikhs come from the Punjab where women are not given equal rights with men.
- In Punjabi society girls are regarded as the property of their father and then their husbands.
- It is difficult to change cultural attitudes and some Sikhs believe that culture is part of religion.
- Most Sikhs with this attitude do not read the scriptures, nor know about the lives and teachings of the Gurus.

Woman is man's other half.

Bhai Gurdas, a seventeenth century Sikh Scholar

Do you think these Sikh women have a religious or cultural attitude to their role in religion?

Questions

b Choose one religion other than Christianity. Do you think women should have equal roles in this religion? Give two reasons for your point of view. **4**

c Choose one religion other than Christianity and explain why some followers give equal roles to women in religion and some do not. **8**

d 'Women should have the same rights as men in religion.'
  i Do you agree? Give reasons for your opinion. **3**
  ii Give reasons why some people may disagree with you. **3**

Exam Tip

d Remember to use the techniques for answering evaluation questions on page 9. Arguments for the statement would be the reasons for the religious attitude in this topic. Arguments against would be the reasons for the cultural attitude in this topic.

SUMMARY

- Some Sikhs believe that men and women are totally equal and should have the same roles in life and religion because this is the teaching of the Gurus.
- Some Sikhs are affected by cultural attitudes and think women should be subordinate to men and not have a role in religion.

Topic 4.4 The United Kingdom as a multi-ethnic society

KEY WORDS

Discrimination – Treating people less favourably because of their ethnicity/gender/colour/class.

Ethnic minority – a member of an ethnic group (race) which is much smaller than the majority group.

Multi-ethnic society – many different races and cultures living together in one society.

Prejudice – believing some people are inferior or superior without even knowing them.

Racism – the belief that some ethnic groups are superior to others.

The United Kingdom has always been a mixed society – Celts, Romans, Angles, Saxons, Jutes, Danes, Vikings, Normans are all ancestors of the British.

In the nineteenth century the United Kingdom built up an overseas empire around the world, leading to small black communities in Bristol, Liverpool and Cardiff.

After the Second World War, a shortage of workers led to many different cultures from the Empire and Commonwealth coming to work in Britain.

Afro-Caribbeans (Africans and West Indians), Indians, Pakistanis, Chinese and Bangladeshis settled in the United Kingdom, many of them having fought in the British forces in the Second World War.

The extension of the European Union led to a large influx of Eastern Europeans. Wars and racial/religious persecutions have led to an increase of asylum seekers.

Even so, in the 2001 Census, only 7.9 per cent of the United Kingdom's population came from **ethnic minorities** (though this percentage changes greatly in different areas), and over half were born and educated in the United Kingdom.

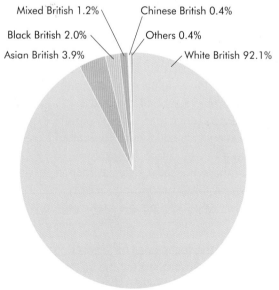

The different ethnicities in the UK, according to the 2001 census.
Source: Census 2001

Traditionally, the man of the family is the provider and protector of women in Hindu families.

The problems of discrimination and racism

Racism is a type of **prejudice** which can cause major problems in a **multi-ethnic society** because of the **discrimination** it leads to. Racist people believe the ethnic group to which they belong to be superior to all other ethnic groups. Religiously prejudiced people believe that everyone who does not believe in their religion is wrong.

Why do you think US President, Barack Obama, is seen by many as a sign that the USA now truly has equal rights?

The problems of discrimination and racism:

- Racially prejudiced employers will not give jobs to certain ethnic groups.
- Religiously prejudiced employers will not give jobs to certain religious groups.
- Prejudiced landlords are likely to refuse accommodation to certain ethnic groups or religions.
- If teachers are prejudiced against certain ethnic minorities or religious groups, they will discriminate against them in their teaching so that those pupils do not achieve the results they should.
- Prejudiced police officers will discriminate against certain ethnic or religious groups, for example by stopping and searching them when they have no real reason for so doing.

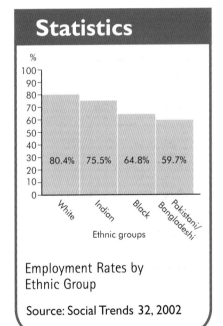

Statistics

Employment Rates by Ethnic Group

Source: Social Trends 32, 2002

Skilled immigrants from Eastern Europe, far from posing a threat, will help to raise wages in Britain and boost exports, economists predict ... Eastern European countries have plenty of skilled people with post-school education and training.

The Times, 5 April 2004

The effects of discrimination and racism

Discrimination and racism have very bad effects for a multi-ethnic society:

- If certain groups feel that they are being treated unfairly by society, then they will begin to work against that society.
- Some politicians believe that young black people turn to crime because they feel they will not be able to get good well-paid jobs because of discrimination.
- Some politicians believe that young Muslims have been turning to extremist Islamic groups because they feel they have no chance of success in a prejudiced British society.
- Racism and discrimination can lead to groups like the BNP (British National Party) stirring up hatred and violence.

A performer in the Notting Hill Carnival in London.

If a multi-ethnic society is to function well, it must treat all its members fairly, and give equal opportunities to all its members.

The benefits of living in a multi-ethnic society

Multi-ethnic societies bring far more benefits than problems:

- People of different ethnic groups and nationalities will get to know and like each other, and probably intermarry, bringing more peace.
- More progress will be made in a multi-ethnic society because new people will bring in new ideas and new ways of doing things.
- Life is more interesting with a much greater variety of food, music, fashion and entertainment.
- A multi-ethnic society helps people to live and work in a world of multi-national companies and economic interdependence between all nations.

How does this crowd celebrating Chinese New Year in London's Chinatown in 2007 show the UK as a multi-ethnic society?

Questions

b Do you think we need laws against racism?
  Give two reasons for your point of view. **4**
c Explain why discrimination and racism cause problems in a multi-ethnic society. **8**
d 'Prejudice and discrimination should be banned.'
  i Do you agree? Give reasons for your opinion. **3**
  ii Give reasons why some people may disagree with you. **3**

Exam Tip

c 'Explain' means give reasons. To answer this question you should use four effects of discrimination and racism. Your answer should be four short paragraphs. For tips on Quality of Written Communication, look at page 3.

SUMMARY

- Britain has many ethnic minorities and so is a multi-ethnic society.
- Multi-ethnic societies have many benefits, such as advancing more quickly because they have a greater variety of ideas.
- A multi-ethnic society needs equal opportunities and treatment to work, and prejudice and discrimination cause major problems in such a society because they do not treat everyone equally.

Topic 4.5 Government action to promote community cohesion in the United Kingdom

Nothing in this Part [of the Act] shall be read, or given effect, in a way which prohibits or restricts discussion, criticism or expressions of antipathy, dislike, ridicule, insult or abuse of particular religions ... Therefore the new offence has an even higher threshold than the race hatred offence, recognising that religious beliefs are a legitimate subject of vigorous public debate.

Home Office Press Release
1 October 2007

Community cohesion may have prevented atrocities like the 7 July 2007 London bombings.

A multi-ethnic society needs to promote **community cohesion** in order to remove the problems of prejudice, discrimination and racism. The UK government promotes community cohesion by:

- giving money to groups which are working for community cohesion
- making community cohesion part of the national education curriculum
- paying for research into the best ways of achieving community cohesion
- appointing cabinet ministers, judges, etc. from ethnic minorities
- passing the Race Relations Act which makes it unlawful to discriminate against anyone because of race, colour, nationality, ethnic or national origins; or to stir up racial hatred
- passing the Crime and Disorder Act which allows more severe punishment for offences which involve racial or religious hatred
- passing the Racial and Religious Hatred Act which makes it an offence to use threatening words or behaviour about religious beliefs or lack of belief
- establishing the Equality and Human Rights Commission which promotes equality and human rights for all, and works to get rid of discrimination and to build good relations
- making sure that the Labour Party, the Conservative Party and the Liberal Democrat Party oppose racism and encourage members of ethnic minorities to become MPs.

Why community cohesion is important

Community cohesion is important for all multi-ethnic and **multi-faith societies** because:

- Without community cohesion, different groups have different ideas about what society should be like and this can lead to violence.

- A lack of community cohesion in Oldham, Burnley and Bradford led to racially/religiously motivated street rioting in 2001 caused by different groups leading separate lives, ignorance about other communities and weak local leadership and policing.
- The 7/7 bombers were British citizens who had lost their sense of allegiance to Britain.
- In countries without community cohesion (such as Iraq, Kosovo, Kashmir) violence becomes a way of life.
- Lack of community cohesion makes it impossible for people to work together as modern societies need.

Cohesion is therefore about:

- how to avoid the bad effects of prejudice and discrimination
- how to encourage different groups to work together
- how to ensure respect for others whilst building up loyal citizens of the same society.

SUMMARY

The government is promoting community cohesion in the UK by passing laws against racism and discrimination, and by making community cohesion part of the national curriculum. Community cohesion is important because without it a multi-ethnic society could become violent and divided.

Questions

b Do you think the government should spend money promoting community cohesion?
Give two reasons for your point of view. **4**

c Explain how the government is trying to promote community cohesion. **8**

d 'Promoting community cohesion is the most important thing a government can do in a multi-ethnic society.'
  i Do you agree? Give reasons for your opinion. **3**
  ii Give reasons why some people may disagree with you. **3**

Exam Tip

c 'Explain' means give reasons. To answer this question you should use four government actions from this topic, and for each action explain how it should improve community cohesion. Your answer should be four short paragraphs. For tips on Quality of Written Communication, look at page 3.

In almost every one of the Commonwealth's 53 nations there are schools distinguished by names like King's, Queen's, Bishop's ... We studied Tudors and Stuarts. We produced **Julius Caesar, Richard II** *and* **Much Ado About Nothing** *... But there was something else we valued even more ... We believed that a liberal democratic state in which individual freedom is assured, and where talent, and hard work are rewarded, was superior to any alternative ... on offer. We were taught that, whatever your background you owed something to your country – and that all traditions could and should play a part in nation building. That we would all have, somehow, to share this space.*

... Our planet has never been more in need of that shared set of values and that common sentiment of toleration than today ... (the) Equality and Human Rights Commission has (a duty) to make sure that people who are very different can live together. It is integral to our mandate of reducing inequality, promoting human rights, strengthening good relations.

From a speech by Trevor Phillips, Head of the Equality and Human Rights Commission, January 2008

Topic 4.6 Why Christians should help to promote racial harmony

Christians should try to promote (bring about) **racial harmony** because:

1 In the Parable of the Good Samaritan, Jesus showed that races who hated each other (as did the Jews and Samaritans) should love each other as neighbours. The Good Samaritan helped the Jew who was attacked as his neighbour, showing that Christians should treat all races as their neighbours.

> 'Which of these three do you think was a neighbour to the man who fell into the hands of robbers?' The expert in the law replied, 'The one who had mercy on him,' Jesus told him, 'Go and do likewise.'
>
> Luke 10:36–37

Vincent Van Gogh's painting, *The Good Samaritan*. How does the Parable of the Good Samaritan encourage Christians to promote racial harmony?

> I now really understand ... that God has no favourites, but that anybody of any nationality who fears him and does what is right is acceptable to him.
>
> Acts 10:34

2 Jesus treated people of different races equally (e.g. a Samaritan woman, a Roman centurion and the black African who helped him carry his cross).

3 St Peter had a vision from God, telling him not to discriminate because God has no favourites among the races. St Peter promoted racial harmony, and he was the greatest disciple, so Christians should follow his example.

> You are all sons of God through faith in Christ Jesus, for all of you who were baptised into Christ have clothed yourselves with Christ. There is neither Jew nor Greek, slave nor free, male and female, for you are all one in Christ Jesus.
>
> Galatians 3:26–28

4   St Paul taught that all races are equal in Christ since God created all races in his image.

5   The Christian Church has members from every race. Over 50 per cent of the world is Christian and 70 per cent of Christians are non-white.

6   All the Christian Churches have made statements recently condemning any form of racism or racial discrimination.

> *The Church rejects as foreign to the mind of Christ, any discrimination against men or harassment of them because of their race, colour, condition of life, or religion.*
>
> **Declaration on the Relationship of the Catholic Church to non-Christians**

> *Respect for the humanity we share with each and every neighbour is the only basis for a peaceful and good society. Any attack on the dignity and human rights of any racial or religious group damages all of us.*
>
> **From the Churches Together letter to the press, May 1998**

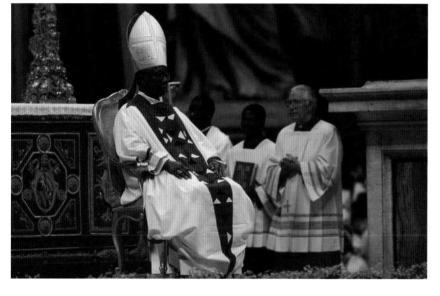

Cardinal Francis Arinze of Nigeria, suggested by some as a possible Pope, a sign of racial harmony in the Christian Church.

Questions

b   Do you think Christians should help to promote racial harmony? Give two reasons for your point of view.   **4**

c   Explain why Christians should help to promote racial harmony.   **8**

d   'If everyone were religious, there would be no racism.'
   i   Do you agree? Give reasons for your opinion.   **3**
   ii   Give reasons why some people may disagree with you.   **3**

Exam Tip

b   You should already have thought about this, and you just have to give two reasons for your opinion. For example, if you agree with Christians promoting racial harmony, you could use two reasons from this topic.

SUMMARY

Christians should promote racial harmony because of the teachings of the Bible and the Church against racism, and because they should follow the example of Jesus.

Topic 4.7.1 Islam and racial harmony

The hajj is an example of racial harmony in Islam. Over two million Muslims of all races and colours gather in Makkah.

All mankind is from Adam and Eve, an Arab has no superiority over a non-Arab, nor a non-Arab has any superiority over an Arab; also a white has no superiority over a black, nor a black has any superiority over a white... Learn that every Muslim is a brother to every Muslim and that the Muslims constitute one brotherhood.

The Prophet Muhammad in his Last Sermon, 9 Dhul Hijjah 632

SUMMARY

Muslims should promote racial harmony because Islam teaches that racism is wrong because of the teachings of the Qur'an and the example of Muhammad.

There are many reasons why Muslims should try to promote racial harmony:

- The Qur'an teaches that God created the whole of humanity from one pair of humans. Therefore all races are related and none can be regarded as superior.
- In his final sermon, Prophet Muhammad said that every Muslim is a brother to every other Muslim, and so there should be no racism among Muslims.
- Muslims should follow the example of Muhammad who promoted racial harmony. For example, his first prayer caller was a black African Muslim, whereas Muhammad was an Arab.
- Islam itself has members in most ethnic groups and most countries around the world. It is the world's second largest religion.
- Islam teaches that all Muslims form one brotherhood, the **Ummah**. This means that all Muslims, whatever their race, should regard each other as brothers and sisters.
- Islam is against any form of racism. Muslim leaders and local mosques work with various groups to promote racial harmony in the United Kingdom.

Questions

b Do you think it is important for religious people to work for racial harmony? Give two reasons for your point of view. **4**

c Choose one religion other than Christianity and explain why the followers of that religion should help to promote racial harmony. **8**

d 'Nothing does more for racial harmony than religion.'
   i Do you agree? Give reasons for your opinion. **3**
   ii Give reasons why some people may disagree with you. **3**

Exam Tip

d Remember to use the techniques for answering evaluation questions on page 9. Arguments for the statement would be the reasons for Muslims and/or Christians promoting racial harmony. Arguments against would be religious people who are racist, and groups that claim to be religious but are racist, for example, the Ku Klux Klan in the USA claimed to be Christian but used violence against black people; also the Dutch Reformed Church in South Africa taught that black people should not be treated equally.

Topic 4.7.2 Judaism and racial harmony

Although most followers of Judaism are also members of the Jewish race (though not necessarily the same ethnic group), Judaism promotes racial harmony because:

- The Torah teaches racial harmony. It shows that all humans can be traced back to Adam and Eve and so they must all be brothers and sisters.
- Most rabbis teach that as God is one, so humanity is one because it was created by the one God.
- There is a lot of teaching in the Tenakh about how God cares for the oppressed and wants his people to bring justice to the world.
- The Jewish people have been given a special responsibility by God to show God's laws to the rest of humanity. Part of this responsibility must be promoting racial harmony.
- There have been many racist attacks on Jews over the past two thousand years, including the Holocaust during the Second World War when the Nazis tried to destroy the whole Jewish race. This makes it impossible for most Jews to regard racism as anything but evil.

> Adam named his wife Eve, because she would become the mother of all the living.
>
> **Genesis 3:20**

> Do not abhor an Edomite, for he is your brother. Do not abhor an Egyptian, because you lived as an alien in his country.
>
> **Deuteronomy 23:7**

> When an alien lives with you in your land, do not ill-treat him. The alien living with you must be treated as one of your native-born.
>
> **Leviticus 19:33–34**

An Ethiopian Jew emigrating to Israel.

Questions

b Do you think it is important for religious people to work for racial harmony? Give two reasons for your point of view. **4**

c Choose one religion other than Christianity and explain why the followers of that religion should help to promote racial harmony. **8**

d 'Nothing does more for racial harmony than religion.'
  i Do you agree? Give reasons for your opinion. **3**
  ii Give reasons why some people may disagree with you. **3**

Exam Tip

d Remember to use the techniques for answering evaluation questions on page 9. Arguments for the statement would be the reasons for Jewish people and/or Christians promoting racial harmony. Arguments against would be religious people who are racist, and groups that claim to be religious but are racist, for example, the Ku Klux Klan in the USA claimed to be Christian but used violence against black people; also the Dutch Reformed Church in South Africa taught that black people should not be treated equally.

SUMMARY

Jewish people should promote racial harmony because Judaism teaches that racism is wrong because of the teachings of the Torah and Jewish experiences in the Holocaust.

Topic 4.7.3 Hinduism and racial harmony

Many different races are members of Hare Krishna.

There are many reasons why Hindus should try to promote racial harmony:

- Hindus believe that every soul is an actual or potential part of the divine (Brahman). So every soul must be of equal value, whatever their race or colour.
- The Indian Hindus suffered from racist treatment when they were ruled by the Moghul, and then the British, Empires. This treatment has led Hindu leaders to work for racial harmony.
- Although the majority of Hindus are from India, there are many different ethnic groups in India. Gandhi, who led the struggle for Indian independence, taught that the different racial and ethnic groups in India must work and live together as equals.
- There are many people from ethnic groups outside India who are converting to Hinduism, and they are all treated as equals by Indian Hindus.
- Hinduism is opposed to racism and racial discrimination in any form. Hindus work with many other groups in the United Kingdom to promote racial harmony.

> *When ... religion creates no barriers between man and man, then the denial of freedom and equality to all human beings is not only politically unjust, but spiritually sinful.*
>
> **The Harijan Journal**

SUMMARY

Hindus should promote racial harmony because they believe that every soul is a part of Brahman and so everyone should be treated equally.

Questions

b Do you think it is important for religious people to work for racial harmony? Give two reasons for your point of view. **4**

c Choose one religion other than Christianity and explain why the followers of that religion should help to promote racial harmony. **8**

d 'Nothing does more for racial harmony than religion.'
  i Do you agree? Give reasons for your opinion. **3**
  ii Give reasons why some people may disagree with you. **3**

Exam Tip

d Remember to use the techniques for answering evaluation questions on page 9. Arguments for the statement would be the reasons for Hindus and/or Christians promoting racial harmony. Arguments against would be religious people who are racist, and groups that claim to be religious but are racist, for example, the Ku Klux Klan in the USA claimed to be Christian but used violence against black people; also the Dutch Reformed Church in South Africa taught that black people should not be treated equally.

Topic 4.7.4 Sikhism and racial harmony

Although most followers of Sikhism are also ethnic Punjabis, Sikhism is opposed to racism and racial discrimination in any form. Sikhs work to promote racial harmony because:

- The Gurus all opposed the **caste system** and treated all groups as equals.
- Guru Nanak emphasised that anyone from any race can come to salvation.
- In every Sikh act of worship everyone, whatever their race, eats from the same bowl, and sits together in the langar.
- Sikhism teaches that because there is only one God who created the whole of humanity, humanity must also be one.

People ignore 'untouchables' as they pass by in the streets. Why might Sikhs regard this as a form of racism?

> In the hereafter, no one is regarded as different from another on grounds of caste.
>
> **Guru Granth Sahib 349**

> Let no one be proud of their birth. We are all born from the same clay.
>
> **Guru Granth Sahib**

> O, my body, God infused divine light in you and you were born into the world.
>
> **Guru Granth Sahib 921**

Questions

b Do you think it is important for religious people to work for racial harmony? Give two reasons for your point of view. **4**

c Choose one religion other than Christianity and explain why the followers of that religion should help to promote racial harmony. **8**

d 'Nothing does more for racial harmony than religion.'
  i Do you agree? Give reasons for your opinion. **3**
  ii Give reasons why some people may disagree with you. **3**

Exam Tip

d Remember to use the techniques for answering evaluation questions on page 9. Arguments for the statement would be the reasons for Sikhs and/or Christians promoting racial harmony. Arguments against would be religious people who are racist, and groups that claim to be religious but are racist, for example, the Ku Klux Klan in the USA claimed to be Christian but used violence against black people; also the Dutch Reformed Church in South Africa taught that black people should not be treated equally.

SUMMARY

Sikhs should promote racial harmony because Sikhism teaches that racism is wrong because of the teachings of the Guru Granth Sahib and the teachings and examples of the Gurus.

Topic 4.8 The United Kingdom as a multi-faith society

Many societies were mono-faith (having only one religion) until the twentieth century. However, Britain has had believers in different faiths for many years – Protestants and Catholics from the sixteenth century, and Jews from the seventeenth century.

This led to laws allowing **religious freedom**. By the middle of the nineteenth century members of any religion were free to worship and had equal political rights.

In the twentieth century Muslims, Hindus, Sikhs, Buddhists and other religions settled in the United Kingdom, so that it became a truly multi-faith society.

The 2001 Census shows which areas of the UK are the most multi-faith:

- the London Borough of Tower Hamlets has the highest percentage of Muslims at 36.4 per cent
- Leicester has the highest percentage of Hindus at 14.3 per cent
- the London Borough of Barnet has the highest percentage of Jews at 14.8 per cent
- Slough has the highest percentage of Sikhs at 9.1 per cent
- the London Borough of Westminster has the highest percentage of Buddhists at 1.3 per cent
- in Birmingham 14.4 per cent of the population are Muslim, 2.9 per cent Sikh, 2 per cent Hindu, 0.3 per cent Buddhist, 0.24 per cent Jewish
- in Bradford 16 per cent of the population are Muslim, 1.1 per cent Sikh, 0.9 per cent Hindu
- in the London Borough of Hounslow, there are 110,657 Christians, 16,064 Hindus, 19,378 Muslims and 18,265 Sikhs. However, many of the non-Christian religions live in the area of Southall.

Statistics

Census facts on religion in England and Wales

Christians
42,558,000 = 72.6%

No religion
8,197,221 = 14%

No answer
4,823,000 = 8.2%

Muslim
1,591,207 = 2.7%

Hindu
558,746 = 0.95%

Sikh
336,040 = 0.57%

Jewish
267,711 = 0.46%

Buddhist
149,237 = 0.25%

Other religions
157,000 = 0.27%

Source: Census 2001, ONS

The benefits of living in a multi-faith society

A multi-faith society has many benefits:

- People can learn about other religions. This can help them to see what religions have in common.
- People from different religions may practise their religion more seriously. This may make people think about how they practise their own religion.
- People may come to understand why different religions believe what they do. This may make people think more seriously about their own beliefs.
- People are likely to become a lot more understanding about and respectful of each other's religions.
- Religious freedom and understanding will exist in a multi-faith society. This may help to stop religious conflicts.
- A multi-faith society may even make some people think more about religion as they come across religious ideas they have never thought about before.

Almost a quarter of the British population did not provide a specific religious preference. This alone suggests that the number of Jews is undercounted. This was not unexpected and, in fact, there are grounds for suggesting that Jews may be more reluctant than others to answer a voluntary question on religion in the census. For historical reasons, many older Jews of Central and Eastern European background are reluctant to co-operate with government-sponsored counts of Jews.

The Institute for Jewish Policy Research findings on the religious results of the 2001 census

These new religious buildings show the multi-faith nature of British society. These pictures show the Shri Swaminarayan Mandir in Neasden and the Tibetan Buddhist Temple of Samye Lings, Dumfriesshire.

Questions

b Do you think it is a good idea to have a lot of different religions in one place? Give two reasons for your point of view. **4**

c Explain why the United Kingdom is often referred to as a multi-faith society. **8**

d 'All societies should be multi-faith societies.'
  i Do you agree? Give reasons for your opinion. **3**
  ii Give reasons why some people may disagree with you. **3**

Exam Tip

c 'Explain' means give reasons. To answer this question you should use the census facts and the facts from different local councils and explain how they show the UK to be a multi-faith society. Your answer should be four short paragraphs. For tips on Quality of Written Communication, look at page 3.

SUMMARY

Britain is a multi-faith society because several religions are practised here and everyone is free to practise their religion. A multi-faith society has many benefits such as religious freedom and the opportunity to find out about, and think more deeply about, different religions.

Topic 4.9 Issues raised for religion by a multi-faith society

KEY WORDS

Interfaith marriage – marriage where the husband and wife are from different religions.

Religious pluralism – accepting all religions as having an equal right to co-exist.

Can it be right to try to convert others when living in a multi-faith society?

Tolerance is so important, and never more so for Jews and Muslims. After September 11, the imam of the local mosque came to say a prayer for peace in Arabic, and I went to the mosque to say a prayer for peace in Hebrew.

Dr J. Romaine, rabbi of Maidenhead (quoted in *The Times*, 31 March 2004)

For a multi-faith society to work, people need to have the same rights regardless of the religion they do or do not belong to (**religious pluralism**). A multi-faith society cannot accept any one religion as being the true one.

Similarly a multi-faith society must have religious freedom. The people living in the society must be free to choose or reject any or all of the religions practised in the society.

This can raise a number of issues for religion:

Conversion

Conversion is an issue because:

1   Many religions see it as their duty to convert everyone because:

   • They believe that their religion is the only true religion.
   • They believe that the only way for the followers of other religions to get to heaven is for them to be converted.
   • Their holy books teach them that they should convert non-believers.

2   Trying to convert other religions can cause major problems because:

   • Treating people differently because of their religion and trying to convert other religions is discriminating against those who do not have the same faith as you.
   • It is impossible to say all other religions are wrong unless you have studied all of them and no one who is trying to convert others has done this.
   • Trying to convert others can lead to arguments and even violence when people are told their religion is wrong.

Bringing up children

A multi-faith society requires everyone (including children) to have religious freedom and be able to choose which religion to follow, or to reject religion. It also requires that children should learn about the different religions in the society. This causes problems for many religious believers because:

- Most religions encourage parents to bring up their children in their religion, and become members of it.
- Most religions teach that only those who follow their religion will have a good life after death. Parents worry what will happen to their children after death if they do not stay in their religion.
- Social and peer pressures compel parents to exert pressure on their children to remain in the faith.
- Children educated in state schools are tempted away from religious lifestyles into the lifestyles of British teenagers.

Interfaith marriages

In a multi-faith society, young people of different faiths are going to meet, fall in love and want to marry. This can raise problems because:

- Often both couples must be members of the same religion to have a religious wedding ceremony.
- There is a question of which religion the children of the marriage will be brought up in.
- There is also the problem of what will happen to the couple after death.
- The parents and relatives of the couple often feel that they have been betrayed.

Unless these issues are dealt with, then religion itself can be working against community cohesion and promoting conflict and hatred.

SUMMARY

A multi-faith society needs to have laws giving equal rights to all religions and to those who have no religion (religious pluralism). However, a multi-faith society can raise problems for religious people in areas such as:

- conversion attempts by other faiths because it is like discrimination
- bringing up children because they may leave their parents' faith
- interfaith marriages because of having to decide which faith the children should be brought up in.

Questions

b Do you think children should be free to choose their own religion? Give two reasons for your point of view. **4**

c Explain why mixed-faith marriages may cause problems. **8**

d 'In a multi-faith society, no religion should try to convert other people.'

   i Do you agree? Give reasons for your opinion. **3**

   ii Give reasons why some people may disagree with you. **3**

Exam Tip

b You should already have thought about this, and you just have to give two reasons for your opinion. For example, if you disagree you could use two reasons from the section on bringing up children.

Topic 4.10 Ways in which religions work to promote community cohesion in the United Kingdom

The different religions in the United Kingdom are beginning to work to promote community cohesion in the following ways:

> Let there be no compulsion in religion.
>
> **Surah 2:256**

> The lamps are different, but the light is the same.
>
> **Rumi, a medieval Iranian Sufi, speaking about different religions**

1 Different religions are beginning to work with other religions to try to discover what is the same in their religions (for example, Judaism, Islam and Christianity believe in the prophets Abraham and **Moses**). From this they work out ways of living together without trying to convert each other. For example, when Pope Benedict XVI addressed a meeting of envoys from the Muslim world in October 2007, he expressed his respect for Muslims and said that the future of the world depends on Christians and Muslims talking and working together.

Pope Benedict XVI meeting Muslim envoys. Do you think it is possible for Christians and Muslims to accept each other's religion?

2 Some religious groups are developing ways of helping **interfaith marriages**.

- Many Protestant Churches and Liberal/Reform Jewish synagogues have developed special wedding services for mixed faith couples.
- The Church of England now has 'Guidelines for the celebration of interfaith marriages in church'.
- Some religious leaders have set up the website www.interfaithmarriage.org.uk to offer help and advice to couples from different religions.

How can you tell this is an interfaith wedding?

All nations form but one community. ... The Catholic Church recognises in other religions that search for the God who is unknown yet near since he gives life and breath and all things and wants all men to be saved.

Catechism of the Catholic Church 842–843

All religions have a common faith in a higher reality which demands brotherhood on earth ... perhaps one day such names as Christianity, Buddhism, Islam, Hinduism will no longer be used to describe men's religious experience.

John Hick (Christian philosopher)

3   The problem of bringing up children is being dealt with in different ways:

- Some Protestant Christian Churches and Liberal/ Reform Jewish synagogues encourage mixed faith parents to bring up their children in both faiths.
- Leaders from the Church of England, Hindu, Sikh, Catholic, Muslim, Jewish and Buddhist faiths have agreed to follow the National Framework on Religious Education so that children in faith schools will now be taught the main religions practised in the United Kingdom.

> Religions are different roads converging to the same point. What does it matter which road we take as long as we reach the same goal? In reality, there are as many different religions as there are individuals.
>
> **Mohandas Gandhi**

> All religions should stand side by side and go hand in hand. They are one family ... they give visions of Truth and Reality. And the real truth of all religion is Harmony.
>
> **His Holiness Pramukh Swami Maharaj (BAPS)**

4. The main way in which religions are trying to promote community cohesion is through working together in special groups.

- There are national groups such as the Inter Faith Network for the UK which was founded in 1987 to promote good relations between people of different faiths in this country (see www.interfaith.org.uk).
- There are also groups in most towns and cities bringing together the different religious groups in an area. For example, the Glasgow Forum of Faiths.
- There are individual places of worship which work together. For example, Father Michael Barnes, parish priest St Anselm's, Southall, says 'Our neighbours next door are Hindus. For the last three years at Diwali, we have gone there for a meal and then gone out into the garden to set off the fireworks.'

The St Mungo Museum is the only museum in the UK dedicated to promoting community cohesion through religion. It is in the grounds of Glasgow Cathedral.

GLASGOW FORUM OF FAITHS DECLARATION

The current world situation has exposed the fragility of interfaith relations and the need for an initiative that helps faith communities to listen and build relationships with each other. There is also an urgent need to show the general public that religion should not be a source of strife and that interfaith activity is worthwhile.

The Forum of Faiths will bring together civic authorities (councillors and council officials) and the leaders of the main faith communities who have subscribed to this Declaration to work together for mutual understanding and the good of the City of Glasgow. We hope the Forum of Faiths will contribute to a better understanding of shared religious values.

The Declaration was signed by the Council leaders, the Strathclyde Police leaders and the Glasgow leaders of the Baha'i faith, the Buddhist faith, the Christian Church of Scotland (like the URC in England), the Christian Roman Catholic Church, the Christian Scottish Episcopal Church (like the Church of England), the Hindu faith, the Jewish faith, the Muslim faith and the Sikh faith.

To recognise the oneness of all humanity is an essential pillar of Sikhism. Some call themselves Hindus, others call themselves Muslims, but humanity worldwide is made up of one race.

Akal Ustal

This Mission is opposite the St Mungo Museum. How does it show the problems of bringing religions together?

Questions

b Do you think different religions should work together in the United Kingdom? Give two reasons for your point of view. **4**

c Explain how different religions are working together to promote community cohesion in the United Kingdom. **8**

d 'It is easy for different religions to work together in the United Kingdom.'
  i Do you agree? Give reasons for your opinion. **3**
  ii Give reasons why some people may disagree with you. **3**

Exam Tip

c 'Explain' means give reasons. To answer this question you should use the facts from this topic, but relate them very clearly to multi-faith society, explaining how the census figures in Topic 4.8 show the United Kingdom to be multi-faith, for example.

SUMMARY

Religions are working for community cohesion in the United Kingdom by:
- working to discover what is the same about religions
- helping with mixed-faith marriages
- making sure that all children learn about different faiths
- joining local and national groups to promote community cohesion.

Topic 4.11 How an issue from religion and community cohesion has been presented in one form of the media

You have to study how *one* issue from religion and community cohesion has been presented in one form of the media. Your issue could be connected with:

- equal rights for women in religion
- problems of discrimination and racism
- equal rights for ethnic minorities
- equal rights for religious minorities
- religion and racial harmony
- issues connected with living in a multi-faith society
- religions working for community cohesion.

You have total choice of the media but it should only be one of the following:

- a soap opera
- a film
- a television drama or documentary
- a radio programme
- a newspaper article in two different types of newspaper, for example, *The Times* and *The Sun*.

If you study a film such as *Bend It Like Beckham*, you must concentrate on the way it portrays Sikhs living in a multi-faith environment.

You must choose carefully so you can answer questions on:

- why the issue is important
- how it was presented
- whether the presentation was fair to religious beliefs
- whether the presentation was fair to religious people.

To do this you must:

1 Select an issue and a form of media.
2 Decide why the issue is important and why you think the producers of the media decided to focus on this issue.
3 Write an outline of how the issue was presented, listing the main events and the way the events explored the issue.
4 Look closely at the way religious beliefs are treated in the presentation of the issue. Use this information to decide whether you think the presentation was fair to religious beliefs.
5 Look closely at the way religious people are treated in the presentation of the issue. Use this information to decide whether you think the presentation was fair to religious people.

Is the Vicar of Dibley's presentation of equal rights for women in religion fair to religious people?

Questions

b Do you think the media present religious people fairly? Give two reasons for your point of view. **4**

c Choose an issue from religion and community cohesion presented in one form of the media and explain whether the presentation was fair to religious people. **8**

d *You are unlikely to be asked an evaluation question on this section as you only have to study one issue in one form of the media.*

Exam Tip

c Briefly summarise the presentation, then explain why some religious people would think the presentation was fair (with reasons) and why others would think it was unfair (with reasons) then decide what you think.

SUMMARY

When studying the presentation of an issue from religion and community cohesion in the media, you must be able to explain why the issue was chosen, how it was presented, whether the presentation treated religious beliefs fairly and whether the presentation treated religious people fairly.

How to answer exam questions

Question A What is racism? 2 marks

The belief that some races are superior to others.

Question B Do people from a different religion have the right to try to convert you?

Give two reasons for your point of view. 4 marks

No I do not think they do because trying to convert followers of other religions when living in a multi-faith society is a type of prejudice and discrimination. Trying to convert other religions is discriminating against those who do not have the same faith as you.

Also trying to convert others can lead to arguments and even violence within a multi-faith society when people are told their religion is wrong.

Question C Explain why Christians should help to promote racial harmony. 8 marks

Christians should help to promote racial harmony because this is the teaching of Jesus, especially in the Parable of the Good Samaritan. Jesus was asked what loving your neighbour meant and he told the parable as a reply. As Samaritans and Jews hated each other and the Samaritan endangered himself to help a Jew, Jesus was clearly showing that no Christian should be racist.

Also St Peter received a vision in which God showed him that all races are equal and must be treated equally.

Finally, all the Christian Churches have made statements in favour of working for racial harmony and Christians should follow the teachings of their Church.

Question D 'Women should have the same rights as men in religion.'

i Do you agree? Give reasons for your opinion. 3 marks

ii Give reasons why some people may disagree with you. 3 marks

i I agree with this because some Protestant Christians would agree with this because they believe that men and women were created totally equal by God. It says in Genesis 1 that God created male and female equally. Also Jesus treated women as his equals and had women disciples, showing that women should have equal rights.

ii Catholic Christians might disagree with me because they think that women cannot be priests. They believe that because Jesus only appointed men as his apostles only men can be priests. They would also argue that the priest represents Jesus at Mass and as Jesus was a man, only male priests can celebrate Mass.

QUESTION A
A high mark answer because it gives a correct definition.

QUESTION B
A high mark answer because an opinion is backed up by two developed reasons.

QUESTION C
A high mark answer because a developed reason for promoting racial harmony (the Good Samaritan) is backed up by two other reasons. A formal style of English is used and there is good use of specialist vocabulary – parable, Jesus, Jews, Samaritans, St Peter, vision, Christian Churches.

QUESTION D
A high mark answer because it states the candidate's own opinion and backs it up with three clear reasons for thinking that women should have the same rights as men. It then gives two reasons with one developed for Catholics disagreeing and believing that only men can be priests.

Glossary

Key words

Abortion the removal of a foetus from the womb before it can survive

Adultery a sexual act between a married person and someone other than their marriage partner

Agnosticism not being sure whether God exists

Assisted suicide providing a seriously ill person with the means to commit suicide

Atheism believing that God does not exist

Civil partnership a legal ceremony giving a homosexual couple the same legal rights as a husband and wife

Cohabitation living together without being married

Community cohesion a common vision and shared sense of belonging for all groups in society

Contraception intentionally preventing pregnancy from occurring

Conversion when your life is changed by giving yourself to God

Discrimination treating people less favourably because of their ethnicity/gender/colour/class

Ethnic minority a member of an ethnic group (race) which is much smaller than the majority group

Euthanasia the painless killing of someone dying from a painful disease

Faithfulness staying with your marriage partner and having sex only with them

Free will the idea that human beings are free to make their own choices

Homosexuality sexual attraction to the same sex

Immortality of the soul the idea that the soul lives on after the death of the body

Interfaith marriage marriage where the husband and wife are from different religions

Miracle something which seems to break a law of science and makes you think only God could have done it

Moral evil actions done by humans which cause suffering

Multi-ethnic society many different races and cultures living together in one society

Multi-faith society many different religions living together in one society

Natural evil things which cause suffering but have nothing to do with humans

Near-death experience when someone about to die has an out-of-body experience

Non-voluntary euthanasia ending someone's life painlessly when they are unable to ask, but you have good reason for thinking they would want you to do so

Nuclear family mother, father and children living as a unit

Numinous the feeling of the presence of something greater than you

Omni-benevolent the belief that God is all-good

Omnipotent the belief that God is all-powerful

Omniscient the belief that God knows everything that has happened and everything that is going to happen

Paranormal unexplained things which are thought to have spiritual causes, for example, ghosts, mediums

Prayer an attempt to contact God, usually through words

Prejudice believing some people are inferior or superior without even knowing them

Pre-marital sex sex before marriage

Procreation making a new life

Promiscuity having sex with a number of partners without commitment

Quality of life the idea that life must have some benefits for it to be worth living

Racial harmony different ethnic groups living together peacefully

Racism the belief that some ethnic groups are superior to others

Re-constituted family where two sets of children (step-brothers and step-sisters) become one family when their divorced parents marry each other

Reincarnation the belief that, after death, souls are reborn in a new body

Religious experience an experience that makes the person having the experience feel the presence of God

Religious freedom the right to practise your religion and change your religion

Religious pluralism accepting all religions as having an equal right to co-exist

Re-marriage marrying again after being divorced from a previous marriage

Resurrection the belief that, after death, the body stays in the grave until the end of the world, when it is raised

Sanctity of life the belief that life is holy and belongs to God

Sexism discriminating against people because of their gender (being male or female)

Voluntary euthanasia ending life painlessly when someone in great pain asks for death

Christian terms

Anoint put oil on

Apostle one of the twelve men Jesus chose to preach the gospel

Apostles' Creed a short statement of what Christians believe

Baptism sacrament of initiation using water to symbolise the cleansing of sin

Baptist a member of the Baptist Church (a Protestant Church that practises believers' baptism)

Born again the belief of some Christians that acceptance of Jesus as a personal saviour brings forgiveness of sins and a second birth in Christ

Catechism a long statement of all the beliefs of the Catholic Church

Catholic member of the Christian Church led by the Pope (Bishop of Rome)

Church of England the national Church led by the Archbishop of Canterbury and the Queen

Confirmation sacrament in which a person confirms the vows made on their behalf at their baptism

Covenant an agreement

Creationism the belief that God created the universe in the way described in the Bible

Creed a summary of Christian beliefs

Eucharist the thanksgiving service using bread and wine (also called Holy Communion)

Evangelical Protestants Protestants who regard the Bible as the absolute word of God and the only authority for Christians

Gospel literally Good News, used for accounts of the life of Jesus (written by Matthew, Mark, Luke, John)

Just war the religious idea that a war can be right in certain circumstances

Liberal Protestants members of the Protestant Churches who interpret the Bible and Christian beliefs in the light of reason and the modern world

Magisterium the Pope and bishops being guided by the Holy Spirit to interpret the Bible and Tradition for Roman Catholics today

Mass Catholic service that includes the Eucharist

Methodist member of the Protestant Church that broke from the Church of England in the eighteenth century under John Wesley

Minister a specially chosen (ordained) leader in Churches that do not have priests (e.g. the Methodist Church)

Missionary person who travels to spread the Christian faith

Moses Jewish leader who was given the Ten Commandments

New Testament 27 books forming the second part of the Christian Bible

Orthodox a member of the Eastern Churches led by Patriarchs that share the faith based on Constantinople

Pentecostal Protestant Churches that emphasise the gifts of the Holy Spirit

Protestant Churches separated from the Catholic and Orthodox Churches by the emphasis on the Bible as the authority for Christians

Sacrament an outward sign of an inward blessing such as baptism and the Eucharist

Salvation being freed from the power of sin and made ready for eternal life

Sin an act against the will of God

St Paul leader of the Early Church who wrote many of the letters in the New Testament

Ten Commandments rules for living given by God to Moses

United Reformed Church (URC) a Protestant Church

Virgin Mary mother of Christ

Vow solemn promise made to God

Hindu terms

Ahimsa non-violence, respect for life

Arti welcoming ceremony in worship

Ashrama a stage of life

Atman the self or soul

Bhagavad Gita the Song of Krishna, one of the most important Hindu scriptures

Brahman the ultimate reality

Caste the idea that people are born into a particular part of society according to their deeds in their last life

Dharma religious duty

Guru a spiritual teacher

Iskcon the International Society for Krishna Consciousness (a Hindu group sometimes known as Hare Krishnas)

Karma actions or deeds, often called the law of cause and effect

Krishna an avatar (descent to earth) of the God Vishnu

Law of Karma the belief that every action has an effect on the state of the soul and the chances of gaining moksha

Laws of Manu an ancient scripture of instructions on how Hindus should live

Mandir a temple

Moksha liberation from the cycle of rebirth

Nirvana the state after moksha about which Hindus have differing ideas

Puja worship

Samsara the eternal cycle of birth, death and rebirth

Shikshapatri of Lord Swaminarayan the book of the teachings of Lord Swaminarayan, founder of the Swaminarayan group (BAPS)

Shiva one of the principal deities of Hinduism

Shrine a focus of worship usually with statues of gods/goddesses

Swami a religious teacher

Swaminarayan a Hindu group also known as BAPS (Worldwide Bochasanwasi Shri Akshar Purushottam Swaminarayan Sanstha)

Upanishads Hindu scriptures that explain the Vedas

Vedas the first Hindu scriptures

Virashaivas a Hindu group following Vishnu

Jewish terms

Bet Din a Jewish court of law

Chuppah canopy used for the wedding ceremony

Get a certificate of divorce

Halakhah the Jewish way of life set out in the mitzvot

Kosher foods permitted for Jews

Liberal Jews a group of Progressive Jews who are more liberal than the Reform Jews

Minyan the number of men over bar mitzvah age required for an Orthodox synagogue (usually 10)

Mitzvot the laws of the Torah

Orthodox Jews those Jews who follow the Torah and halakhah literally

Progressive Jews a term used to describe both Liberal and Reform Jews

Rabbi an ordained Jewish teacher/religious leader

Reform Jews those Jews who think the Torah needs interpreting in the light of the modern world

Shabbat the seventh day, day of rest (sunset Friday to sunset Saturday)

Synagogue building for prayer, worship, education, social activities

Talmud collection of commentaries on the Torah

Ten Commandments rules for living given by God to Moses

Tenakh the Jewish Bible

The Temple the original centre of Judaism in Jerusalem destroyed in 70CE

Thirteen Principles of Faith a summary of Jewish beliefs, written by Maimonides

Torah the five books of Moses containing the Law

Yom Kippur the most solemn and important of the Jewish holidays

Muslim terms

Arafat a plain near Makkah where pilgrims confess their sins when on Hajj

Coitus interruptus generally refers to any extraction of the penis prior to ejaculation during intercourse

Five Pillars the basis of Islam: Shahadah, Salah, Zakah, Sawm (Ramadan), Hajj

Hadith sayings of the Prophet Muhammad

Hajj the annual pilgrimage to Makkah, which is the fifth pillar

Halal food permissible according to Islamic Law

Hijra journey the Prophet Muhammad made from Makkah to Yathrib in 622CE; marks the beginning of the Muslim calendar

Imam prayer leader/community leader

Madrasah evening/weekend school attached to a mosque

Makkah city where Muhammad was born and where the Ka'bah is located

Mosque Muslim place of worship more correctly called a masjid

Prophet Muhammad the final prophet of Islam

Qur'an the holy book of Islam

Ramadan the ninth month of the Islamic year when all Muslims should fast (Sawm)

Salah the five daily prayers, which are the second pillar

Shari'ah the holy law of Islam

Shirk the sin of associating things with Allah

Surah a division of the Qur'an; there are 114 surahs

Ummah the worldwide Muslim community

Zakah a tax Muslims must pay for the poor, which is the third pillar

Sikh terms

Amrit sanctified liquid made of sugar and water

Caste system the system that gave a position in society based on performance in previous lives

Gurdwara Sikh place of worship

Gurmukh God-centred, one who lives by the Guru's teaching

Guru Amar Das the third Sikh Guru

Guru Gobind Singh the tenth Guru and founder of the khalsa

Guru Granth Sahib the Sikh holy book

Guru Nanak the first Guru and founder of Sikhism

Initiation ceremony a ceremony to mark a person joining a religion

Karma actions or deeds, often called the law of cause and effect

Khalsa the community of initiated Sikhs

Langar the gurdwara dining hall and the food served in it

Lavan the wedding hymn

Law of Karma the belief that every action has an effect on the state of the soul and the chances of gaining mukti

Manmukh self-centred, human-centred (opposite of gurmukh)

Mukti liberation from the cycle of birth, death, rebirth

Rahit Maryada the Sikh code of discipline (regulations on how to live as a Sikh)

Samsara the eternal cycle of birth, death and rebirth

Ten Gurus the ten human Gurus beginning with Guru Nanak and ending with Guru Gobind Singh

Index

The Publishers would like to thank the following for permission to reproduce copyright material:

Photo credits

p.1 © Peter Barritt/Alamy; p.2 © Hodder Education; p.4 © Lucien Aigner/Corbis; p.5 © akg-images; p.6 © Polak Matthew/Corbis Sygma; p.7 © Reuters/Corbis; p.8 © Reuters/Corbis; p.11 © *t* Corbis, *b* Jill Watton; p.12 © Royal Observatory, Edinburgh/aatb/Science Photo Library; p13 © Kevin Schafer/Corbis; p.14 © Private Collection/The Stapleton Collection/The Bridgeman Art Library; p.16 © Deep Light Productions/Science Photo Library; p.17 © Wesley Hitt/Alamy; p.19 Punit Paranjpe/Reuters/Corbis; p.20 © Peter Turnley/Corbis; p.21 © STRDEL/AFP/Getty Images; p.22 © Caritas Makeni/CAFOD; p.23 © Bubbles Photolibrary/Alamy; p.24 © Tigeraspect productions; p.25 © Martin Jenkinson/Alamy; p.26 © imagebroker/Alamy; p.27 © Tigeraspect productions; p.29 *l* © Stockfolio/ Alamy, *r* © Jill Watton; p.31 *t* © Digital Art/Corbis, *b* © The London Art Archive/Alamy; p.33 © Jill Watton; p.34 © World Religions Photo Library; p.35 © Reuters/Corbis; p.37 © World Religions Photo Library; p.38 © Christie's Images Ltd.; p.39 © Bojan Brecelj/Corbis; p.40 © World Religions Photo Library; p.41 © World Religions Photo Library; p.43 *l* © Action Press/Rex Features, *r* © Action Press/Rex Features; p. 44 © United Press International, Inc; p.45 © Henry Westheim Photography/Alamy; p.46 © Janine Wiedel/Photofusion; p.47 © Steve Bell/Rex Features; p.48 © Clouds Hill Imaging Ltd./CORBIS; p.49 © Corbis; p.51 © Robert Fishman ecomedia/dpa/ Corbis; p.52 © Robert Nickelsberg/Liaison/Getty Images; p.53 © Dr Najeeb Layyous/Science Photo Library; p.55 © AAP Image/Dave Hunt; p.57 © John Cole/Science Photo Library; p.58 © Bibliotheque Nationale, Paris, France/The Bridgeman Art Library; p.59 © Liba Taylor/Corbis; p.60 © Angelo Hornak/Corbis; p.63 © Akhtar Soomro/epa/Corbis; p.64 © Shahaf Twizer/epa/Corbis; p.65 © David Levenson/Getty Images; p.67 © Victor Watton; p.68 © Photofrenetic/Alamy; p. 69 © Corbis; p.70 © Daniel Hambury/EPA/Corbis; p.72 © RubberBall/Alamy; p.73 © Israel images/Alamy; p.74 © Charles & Josette Lenars/Corbis; p.75 © Circa Religion Photo Library/ Twin Studio; p.76 © Norbert Schaefer/Corbis; p.77 © Images.com/Corbis; p.79 © John R. Rifkin; p.81 © Charles Bowman/ photolibrary.com; p.83 © World Religions Photo Library; p.84 © Fiona Hanson/PA Photos; p.85 © World Religions Photo Library; p.86 © David Grossman/Alamy; p.87 © Bruno Vincent/Getty Images; p.88 © Jim Bourg/Reuters/Corbis; p.89 © C. Lyttle/zefa/Corbis; p.91 © David Levenson/Getty Images; p.92 © Rob Elliott/AFP/Getty Images; p.94 © Bettmann/Corbis; p.96 © Monkey Business Images Ltd/photolibrary.com; p.98 © Emma Wood/Alamy; p.99 © Jennifer Leigh Sauer/Photonica/Getty Images; p.101 © PA Wire/PA Photos; p.102 © Ted Horowitz/Corbis; p.103 © Fox Photos/Getty Images; p.104 © Eduardo Verdugo/AP/PA Photos; p.105 © Peter Southwick/ AP/PA Photos; p.106 © Lynsey Addario/Corbis; p.107 © Kaveh Kazemi/Getty Images; p.108 © Nathan Benn/Alamy; p.109 © Motte JulesABACA/PA Photos; p.110 © ASIM TANVEER/Reuters/Corbis; p.111 © Jewel Samad/AFP/Getty Images; p.112 © World Religions Photo Library; p.113 20th Century Fox/Everett/Rex Features; p.114 © World Religions Photo Library; p.115 © Larry W. Smith/epa/ Corbis; p.116 © Reuters/Corbis; p.117 © Robert Read/Alamy; p.118 © Peter Macdiarmid/epa/Corbis; p.120 Todd Gipstein/Corbis; p.121 © Grzegorz Galazka/Corbis; p.122 © World Religions Photo Library; p.123 © David H. Wells/Corbis; p.124 © Tim Hawkins; Eye Ubiquitous/Corbis; p.125 © Behzad Bernous/Zuma/Corbis; p.127 *l* CIRCA Religion Photo Library/© William Holtby, *r* © CIRCA Religion Photo Library; p.128 © Bob Battersby/BDI Images; p.130 © AP Photo/PA Photos; p.131 © Michael J. Doolittle/ The Image Works; p.132 *l* and *r* © Jill Watton; p.133 © Jill Watton; p.134 © 20th Century Fox/Everett/Rex Features; p.135 © Courtesy of Dawn French.

Acknowledgements
The publishers would also like to thank the following for permission to reproduce material in this book: *The Times*/NI Syndication. The publishers would like to acknowledge use of the following extracts: Alister Hardy Trust, Oxford for an extract from their website www.alisterhardytrust.org.uk; © The Archbishops' Council, the Church Commissioners for England, the Church of England Pensions Board, the Archbishop of Canterbury and the Archbishop of York; Cambridge University Press for an extract from *A New Face of Hinduism* by R. Williams, 1984; Continuum International Publishing Group for extracts from *The Catechism of the Catholic Church*, 2002; Christian Education Movement in partnership with the Churches for extracts from *What the Churches Say*, 2000; Continuum International Publishing Group for an extract from *Themes and Issues in Hinduism* by P. Bowen, 1998; © General Medical Council for an extract from 'Advice to doctors' from *Personal Beliefs and Medical Practice*, 2008; Hodder Arnold for an extract from *Christians in Britain Today* by Denise Cush, 1991; Hodder Arnold for an extract from *Guidelines for Life* by Mel Thompson, 1990; Scripture quotations taken from the HOLY BIBLE, NEW INTERNATIONAL VERSION. Copyright © 1973, 1978, 1984 by International Bible Society. Used by permission of Hodder & Stoughton Publishers, a member of the Hachette Livre UK Group. All rights reserved. 'NIV' is a registered trademark of International Bible Society. UK trademark number 1448790; Hodder & Stoughton for an extract from *If I were God I'd say sorry* by Robert Kirkwood, 1996; Hodder & Stoughton for an extract from *Teach Yourself Sikhism* by W. Owen Cole, 2005; Internet Infidels/www.infidels.org for an extract from *The Case against Immortality* by Keith Augustine, 1997; John Murray for an extract from 'In Westminster Abbey' from *John Betjeman's Collected Poems* by John Betjeman, 1972; The Learning Plant for an extract from *Moral Issues in Judaism* by Arye Forta; Muslim Educational Trust for extracts from *What Does Islam Say?* by I. Hewitt, 1998; Prometheus Books for an extract from *Immortality* by Paul Edwards, 1997; *Science Journal* for an extract from April 2002; SCM for an extract from *Exploration into God* by J.A.T. Robinson, 1967; State University of New York Press for an extract from *Paranormal Experiences and Survival of Death* by C. Becker, 1993; Templeton Foundation Press for an extract from *Science and Creation: The Search for Understanding* by J. Polkinghorne, 2007; UK Statistics Authority website for extracts from www.statistics.gov.uk. Crown Copyright material is reproduced with the permission of the Controller, Office of Public Sector Information (OPSI); Vintage Classics for an extract from *The Severed Head* by Iris Murdoch and Miranda Seymour, 2006.